Beyond the Barbed Wire

'These extraordinary, energetic poems, which grab the reader by the throat both linguistically and morally, are about the power of language itself.'

SUE HUBBARD, *Poetry London*

'Laâbi's finest poems are virtuosic performances, turning political crises into poetic occasions and combining a flair for self-dramatization with stunning verbal inventiveness.'

ROBYN CRESWELL, *Harper's Magazine*

'When it comes to "raising a song of possibilities above the dirge of cruelty", Laâbi is still without rival.'

STACY HARDY, *The Chimurenga Chronic*

Beyond
the Barbed Wire

Selected Poems of
Abdellatif Laâbi

TRANSLATED BY
ANDRÉ NAFFIS-SAHELY

CARCANET

First published in Great Britain in 2016 by CARCANET PRESS LIMITED
Alliance House, Cross Street, Manchester, M2 7AQ / www.carcanet.co.uk

The publisher acknowledges financial support from Arts Council England.

This book has been selected to receive financial assistance from English
PEN's 'PEN Translates!' programme, supported by Arts Council England.
English PEN exists to promote literature and our understanding of it, to
uphold writers' freedoms around the world, to campaign against the per-
secution and imprisonment of writers for the stating of their views, and
to promote the friendly co-operation of writers and the free exchange of
ideas. www.englishpen.org

ABDELLATIF LAÂBI is a poet, novelist, playwright, translator and political activist. He was born in Fez, Morocco in 1942. In the 1960s, Laâbi was the founding editor of *Souffles*, or *Breaths*, a widely-influential literary review that was banned in 1972, at which point Laâbi was imprisoned for eight and a half years. Laâbi's most recent accolades include the Prix Goncourt de la Poésie for his *Oeuvres complètes* (*Collected Poems*) in 2009, and the Académie française's Grand Prix de la Francophonie in 2011. His work has been translated into Arabic, Spanish, German, Italian, Dutch, Turkish and English. Laâbi himself has translated into French the works of Mahmoud Darwish, Abdul Wahab al-Bayati, Mohammed Al-Maghout, Saâdi Youssef, Abdallah Zrika, Ghassan Kanafani, and Qassim Haddad.

ANDRÉ NAFFIS-SAHELY's debut collection of poetry, *The Promised Land*, will be published by Penguin in 2017. He has translated works by Honoré de Balzac, Émile Zola, Alessandro Spina, Rashid Boudjedra, Tahar Ben Jelloun, and Abdellatif Laâbi, among various others.

Contents

From THE WORLD'S EMBRACE (1993)

From WRITE LIFE (2005)

From ANOTHER MOROCCO (2013)

INTERVIEW

*

Introduction

BY JIM MOORE

As soon as I began reading Abdellatif Laâbi in 2013, after a trip to Morocco, his work and life became an obsession and I quickly read everything in English by and about him that I could find. In addition to his poems I discovered his memoir, *The Bottom of the Jar* (Archipelago Books, 2013), which recounts what it was like to grow up in the medina of Fez, a book that is key to understanding Laâbi's working life as a writer. It was in Fez that he began writing in French – the language that was forced upon him in school, but a language to which he gave himself willingly. This split between Arabic and French mirrored a split in his own soul. But like many such tears in the fabric of a life, it has also been a source of much that is most forceful in his writing.

Today when I look at the landscape of poetry being written in English, what I often miss is that sense of absolute necessity in the work, a feeling that 'it is not a matter of choice' for the poet to be writing his or her work. There are significant exceptions to this, of course; for example, many poets of colour publishing today in the United States are writing work that is alive with a need not to be 'smothered by history'. This work is exhilarating, inspiring, and challenging. Nevertheless, the great majority of contemporary poetry feels almost lackadaisical compared to Laâbi's. As if it is a kind of afterthought. It is frequently smart, cleverly self referential; but too often essentially empty. There are certainly exceptions. I think of Jack Gilbert, for example, whose work has that feeling of necessity about it. As does Adrienne Rich's and Larry Levis's, to mention two others.

I wish Abdellatif Laâbi had been with me, some forty years ago, when I was in prison! Laâbi and I were almost exactly the same age, and halfway across the world from each other the Moroccan poet and I were doing time. It was the early 1970s, a period when around the world men and women – even

someone like me, middle class, white and male in America –
could suddenly find themselves at the mercy of political systems
with which it was no longer possible to cooperate. Laâbi was
in prison for over eight years. I was in for ten months. He was
imprisoned for 'radical' literary efforts as an editor and a writer.
I was imprisoned for a specific action. I had turned in my draft-
card and then refused induction into the army. He went through
torture and other difficulties that were not part of my experi-
ence, but still there are parallels that initially drew me to his
work in 2013.

How helpful it would have been for me to have known those
poems forty years earlier. Like Laâbi I was struggling then,
around 1970, with how to put together a life as a poet sur-
rounded by the political and cultural upheaval that was every-
where challenging entrenched institutions and mores. Here is a
small excerpt from one of his early poems, 'Urgent Life', a rich
jumble of a poem, full of chaos and longing, hope and bitter-
ness, love and hate. A young man's poem for sure, and full of a
young man's bravado and confusions, a young man's vulnerabil-
ities. These are the poem's last lines, their jaggedness reflecting
the jaggedness and uncertainty of the times:

I know my path
                    etched on the solstice
but what have we
                    what do we suffer from
rush so that I may watch
                            so I may paraphrase your mutism
hey cadavers
            I bet you've lost the power of speech

when
        vortex
                earth
                    the predicted disaster
we'll no longer make head nor tail of it all

little cry of Nagasaki
little guerilla from the Caribbean
leave me now to write
                    the most dreadful of love songs

That last line – 'the most dreadful of love songs' – might well
be the best description of many of the strongest poems ever
written, from Sappho's fragments to the *Iliad*, from Whitman
and Dickinson to Miłosz and Szymborska, Jack Gilbert to Kevin
Young.

                              *

While I was in prison I discovered that the inmates there kept a
hidden book. It was completely illegal. It would have subjected
them to the punishment of spending more time in prison had it
been discovered. In it they had written out poems by hand that
mattered to them. I was surprised. I hadn't quite understood that
poetry doesn't only matter to people with college educations;
that it is a medium that those in trouble turn to instinctively. As
Breyten Breytenbach wrote in his foreword to *Rue du Retour*,
Laâbi's prison memoir, Laâbi had no choice, while in prison,
but to write poetry. 'To be in prison', writes Breytenbach – who
also spent eight years as a political prisoner in Apartheid South
Africa, from 1975 to 1982 – 'is to be buried alive. The poet's cell
is a tomb. [...] He writes [...]. It is not even a matter of choice.
[...] *not writing* would mean being smothered by *history*. Silence is
death by default.'

  To pick up most poetry magazines today in the United States
and Great Britain is to wonder at how little of it could possibly
matter to a reader in need, the way my fellow inmates in prison
were in need of the poems they inscribed in that notebook. All of
us – whether we know it or not – are in need of poetry at certain
points in our lives in this essential way. Poetry has often been the
immediate response to overwhelming conditions, whether those
conditions are personal in nature or political or both.

  Abdellatif Laâbi was born in 1942 and raised, as I men-
tioned, in the medina of Fez. Fez is still the biggest and oldest

continuously-lived-in city in the world that is not open to automobiles or trucks. As such it feels enclosed, an enclosure which at one moment seems like a privileged bubble, at another like an iron cage. Laâbi's father worked as a saddle-maker in the medina. Both of his parents were uneducated and illiterate. Here's what he has to say about them in an interview with Christopher Schaefer (included in the present volume):

> What pushed me to write? What was the trigger? More and more, the image of my mother imposes itself on me, because she was a woman who had a rich language, full of images, and a great sense of humour. She was often angry at her condition, and it was by listening to her speak that perhaps – and I say perhaps – the desire to write was born in me. So, there is this homage, of course, to that woman who had eleven children, three of whom died – so eight children: three brothers and four sisters who survived. The ten of us lived in a small house of two rooms. My father was a simple craftsman who worked his entire life. My mother worked for us her entire life. It seemed they were almost slaves in our service, so that we could eat, so that we could be clothed, and so that we could go to school. All of that touches me very deeply – to see a man and a woman at that moment in time, in their condition, illiterate – who spent their entire life for us. And that's why they appear not just in *The Bottom of the Jar*, but also in other books of mine.

In the fifties and sixties, Laâbi became involved in the political unrest – its hopes and angers – which swept through North Africa and many other places in the world. In 1966 he was one of the founding editors of *Souffles* (*Breaths*), a magazine that was shut down by the Moroccan government. Though it only lasted until 1972, to this day it remains a touchstone for the hopes of that time throughout the Arab world, its possibilities and its disappointments. Subsequently, Laâbi spent his years in prison, partly due to his work with *Souffles*, a time which he has written movingly about both in poetry and prose, most notably in his prison memoir. Finally released from prison in 1980, three years later he went into voluntary exile in France where he still lives, though he often returns to Morocco. Laâbi retains his status as the leading poet in Morocco, as well as a guiding cultural and political figure, known for his independence, his honesty, his passion for freedom: his ability not just to survive, but to thrive against all odds.

Laâbi's poetry has gone through many iterations, which is only natural for someone who has been writing for more than forty years, not to speak of living through a political and cultural history filled with so much uncertainty, moments of sudden hope and much longer periods of fear and discouragement. Looking back in American history, Walt Whitman lived a somewhat parallel life in a period also filled with turbulence, fear, and deep grief. His work reflects the terrible realities that he witnessed and went through first-hand during the American Civil War. Whitman's poems were deepened by these experiences, grew darker because of them, but never lost their belief in life's possibilities, never became too far removed from life's joys and mysteries. And despite periods of intense discouragement, Whitman often returned to his belief in America's potential.

In Laâbi's case, the early poetry is filled with passion and outrage, with bitterness and love. It frequently moves in a surrealistic way that adds to its tonal unsettledness and uprootedness, an uprootedness that prefigures, in moving ways, Laâbi's own literal unrootedness that began about a decade later when he was finally released from prison. He who had lived the most grounded life imaginable as he was growing up in the medina of Fez would have to go into exile in order to survive. One of his best-known poems from this period is the long poem 'Race', which begins in a way that states starkly the situation in which Laâbi and his fellow artists in Morocco found themselves:

it is we who are alone   emptied   outflanked   at the foot of the
Whispering-walls of true lament surrounding us above and
below
With the mark of disaster   Now denounced   Our vampire
reputations

Facing the world of Reason   Law   and Edicts
stuffed into bruised-body bags   In dead-end deserts
On the brink of depression and suicide

attuned to solitude [...]

As the poem continues it grows more and more desperate, more and more urgent, setting out in relentless and vivid details, in jarring metaphors and outrageous juxtapositions, how it felt almost fifty years ago to be living through a desperate and desperately difficult time. The poem was begun in 1965 and finished in 1967 when Laâbi and his friends were isolated from much of the rest of the world while at the same time connected to the spirit of revolution that was the hallmark of that period.

As Laâbi grows older, his poetry sometimes feels more sombre than in the early work, though by no means always. His strongest poems, such as 'The Earth Opens and Welcomes You', an elegy for another poet written in the 1990s, often combine elements of both ode and elegy. 'The Earth Opens and Welcomes You' is calmer than many of the earlier poems. Yes, the poem is about the earth opening to welcome a fellow poet who has died (who in fact was murdered by extremists), but it is also welcoming in a powerful second sense: the earth welcomes the living within this poem, and there is a keen sense of gratitude for that welcoming. In this way, the poem reminds me of another great ode which is at the same time an elegy, the Turkish poet Nâzım Hikmet's 'Things I Didn't Know I Loved'. Written after his own experience as a political prisoner, Hikmet's poem has the same calm and melancholy spirit as Laâbi's, while still expressing a fierce love of life. In this amazing passage, Laâbi creates an alchemical moment, combining grief and joy to create a third thing, an alloy stronger than either one of these emotions alone:

The earth opens
and welcomes you
You're naked

And she's more naked than you
You're both beautiful
in that silent embrace
where hands can restrain themselves
and steer clear of violence
where the butterfly of the soul
avoids this semblance of light
to go in search of its origins

The later poems are sometimes mysterious in nature, as well as
political, humorous, and grief-stricken, and have a feel of exile
about them (as Robyn Creswell points out in his essay about
Laâbi)* that is often at the heart of ancient Chinese poetry, a
poetry which itself was frequently written in exile.

   And this leads us to Laâbi's state of mind now. In the afore-
mentioned interview with Schaefer he is steadfast in his belief
in the necessity of continuing to fight for freedom of all kinds,
cultural, political and artistic. Such a call might seem born of
optimism but, as best I can judge, his later poems tell a darker
story. He has spent his life seeing the possibilities for freedom he
had hoped for as a young man – freedom from the French but
also from home-grown tyrants and religious fanatics – failing
again and again. In spite of the Arab Spring, it is difficult not to
see the region as a whole as having been beaten down in many
different ways. Laâbi's poetry reflects this, not just in its anger
and occasional bitterness, but in its quiet dignity. Here are the
final lines from 'The Earth Opens and Welcomes You', lines
that not only stand beautifully as an epitaph for his dead friend,
but which also point the way forward for Laâbi as he ages:

Before you left
you left your office in order
neatly arranged

* Robyn Creswell, 'Winds of Revolt', in *Harper's Magazine*, November 2013.

You switched off the lights
and on stepping out
you looked at the sky
which was almost painfully blue
You gracefully smoothed your moustache
and said to yourself:
only cowards
think that death is the end

Sleep well my friend
Sleep the sleep of the righteous
Rest well
from your dreams too
Let us shoulder the burden a little

*

Morocco's struggle for freedom – not just to obtain it but to preserve it – reflects, in a more dramatic and clearly-etched way, similar struggles across the globe, including in the United States and the rest of the English-speaking world. The high hopes of the 1960s and early 70s – hopes for racial and gender equality, for economic parity – have been eroded, and that's putting it mildly. Yes, there are hopeful signs, at least in the literary world – again I would point to the work by poets and writers of colour – but for the most part it feels as if the post-industrial corporate engine has taken up almost all of the cultural and psychic space. Perhaps we need another magazine like the one Laâbi helped to start.

In an essay about poetry and politics, Seamus Heaney wrote about the poet's vocation almost as if he had Laâbi in mind:

In the modern era, the sense of [a poet's] visitation and rededication will often derive from meetings and occasions which are [...] bathed in an uncanny light, occasions when the poet has been, as it were, unhomed, has experienced the *unheimlich*.

[...] The poet typically comes away from such encounters with a renewed sense of election, surer in his or her vocation. What is being enacted or recalled is usually an experience of confirmation, of the spirit coming into its own, a door being opened or a path being entered upon. Usually also the experience is unexpected and out of the ordinary, in spite of the fact that it occurs in the normal course of events, in the everyday world. A strange thing happens. A spot of time becomes a spot of the timeless, becomes, in effect, one of 'the hiding places of (the poet's) power.' *

What began in the 1950s and came to a head in the 1960s and 70s all around the world was that 'in the normal course of events' a door opened into the 'unexpected', opened into the 'timeless' because of cultural and political upheavals that abruptly altered people's lives, 'unhomed' them, challenged and inspired them. Some poets at that time were transfigured by these events, unhomed forever, and set on their path. Thus Abdellatif Laâbi, the son of illiterate and unschooled parents, raised in the heart of the enclosed world of the medina in Fez, found his life altered forever. It became a necessity for him to write: it was his only way to deal with being unhomed.

When I was twenty-six years old and trying, unsuccessfully, to convince myself that I wasn't terrified about going to prison, I wrote a letter to my draft board – the board that had the power to see to it that I went to prison or stay out of it – in which I quoted from Walt Whitman's famous preface to the 1855 edition of *Leaves of Grass*:

This is what you shall do: Love the earth and sun and the animals, despise riches, give alms to everyone that asks, stand up for the stupid and crazy [...] go freely with powerful uneducated persons and with the young and with the mothers of families, [...] re-examine all you have been told at school or church or in

* Seamus Heaney, 'Apt Astonishment', in *The Hudson Review*, Spring 2008.

any book, dismiss whatever insults your own soul, and your very flesh shall be a great poem and have the richest fluency not only in its words but in the silent lines of its lips and face and between the lashes of your eyes and in every motion and joint of your body.

Laâbi, as much as any poet of whom I'm aware, has instinctively followed Whitman's advice here; somehow, the way the world impinged on his fate – as a Moroccan and simply as a human being – actually made him a stronger poet. It is challenging and heartening to read a poet who has been 'welcomed by earth'. In turn, we as readers feel welcomed ourselves. The restlessness of Laâbi's spirit – by turns melancholy and joyous, hopeful and forlorn – is quintessentially the spirit of our times. In the face of the chaos through which Laâbi has lived, what's remarkable is his grace, as well as a lightly-worn dignity, which is all the more moving for its lightness. Though I have drawn parallels to other poets in this introduction, today Laâbi stands virtually alone, having survived terrors unimaginable to most of us. The history of our times has been played out on his body, and transfigured by his spirit into the poems in this remarkable collection.

This new selection of Abdellatif Laâbi's work, gathered from many years of writing and so beautifully translated by André Naffis-Sahely, takes the reader through the many twists and turns of Laâbi's life, at times a life full of drama and despair, at other times a life seemingly lived at one remove. If Laâbi is a political poet – and he certainly is – he is also a poet of great solitude and loneliness. All of this, thanks to this generous and well-chosen selection of his work, is available to us now in English.

*

JIM MOORE is a poet who lives in Minneapolis, Minnesota. His new and selected book of poems, *Underground*, was published by Graywolf Press in 2014.

Beyond the Barbed Wire

Selected Poems

FROM

The Reign of Barbarism

(1976)

The Eye of the Talisman

everything dies
the patched-up brain down in the catacombs

        dies

dies
   the logos of cities
reason dies
crushed under the weight of wrinkles
without any help from one's hands
the grey brain of gloominess dies

      dies

the night when rosary beads are counted

       draws near

for the return of dawn
which the sphinxes prophesied

     even though the return is impossible

they too have grown old now
exhausted by their alliance

    with the wind

right now
I am searching for a new language

     for my tribe's

that isn't some bastardised creole
hurricanes of argan trees

    come to bolster my ranks

a yoke of yellow wasps

    around my throat of earth

it's my dreadful lucidity

like a mirror
                 grown rusty with memories
which History comes thumping against
now I know the kind of powers I have
the peoples that run through my language
when a night of flames
                       builds a silence
I write lullabies
             by dint of hammer blows

my dreadful lucidity
tuned my voice
             to the rhythm of caravans
my dreadful lucidity
sculpted an epoch for me
                  the size of a desert

right now
          I must regurgitate
                 all the layers of narcotics
and fumes of manure
              rational words are as weak as a herbal infusion
I throw out all the books that taught me pride

here I stand
          right here
dressed in the fleece of the night
                  armed with wasps
with that smell of muscles
like a camel's carcass
that's ready to leap onto the road

in a single cry

come and see if my breasts
                              aren't blooming with curses
if only they left me a few veins
or a few nerves
                    or even just a finger
so I could re-trace on my parchment
a new theory of cosmic origins
                              in all the harmoniousness of its
                                                            elements

listen to languages collide
                              inside my mouth
the thirst of births
listen to sweat splash
                        under my armpits
the flexing of biceps
propelled by my inner wildlife
                              leapt out of caves
bloodied quill
                  my head on every wall
the galloping of my breath
spews out planets
                  in its eruptions

here I am
            torrential in my flood
working around bends and corners
the forgotten craters in my incandescence
I Atlas

zebra-striped by the sun
of diurnal tribes
collecting in my falls and ravines
the impatient foam of a coming tomorrow
ask the vultures what my venom tastes like
the callousness of claws
my prison bars of curses
I am a proclaimer
edifying to insurrection
a kingdom

don't look for me in your archives
frightened by my denunciations
what I am you will not find in words
instead look for me in your entrails
when fugitive verses
twist your guts
look for me in the urine of fevers
down the malarial alleyways
there
in the mud of cataracts
destroy my outlawed names
stomp on the spells I radiate
but at my call
smash the jars of honey
slash the throats of the black bulls on the thresholds of mosques
feed thousands and thousands of beggars
then I will come
spit in your mouth
burst your tumours
cure you of your ancestral sufferings
still I prefer you
and the straightness of your ploughs

my rough-handed brothers
my deep-slumbering brothers

come
     cast down
             thrown overboard
a stranger to the orbit of planets
between heaven and nothingness
sprung
     from whimsy
             at the beginning of the word
I know nothing about the laws of gravity
               of the mathematics of
                 revolutions
arab
     berber
          but most importantly, human
yet one who bears a mark
          and a voice
             that are unchangeable

come from your tomorrows
          gravedigger of ruins
whose burden I won't carry
          the mistakes of the night
but instead
     freely make the door knockers clang
so that each threshold
          will yield its algorithm

yes
    I'm asleep
atop a mountain of salt
an ear listening to the wheel of time
I let my arms grow
                    to ripen an awakening
I laugh yes I laugh in my dream
look at my eyelids
which caravan-masters inseminate with germs
and my terrifying eye
                    exacting
                        like an hourglass

Glory to Our Torturers

Just between us
                    the truth
swear to me you won't believe me
we are waiting
for a wheel to break apart inedible flesh
or for an eye to go blind simply for having witnessed
no predator will come stitch up the C-sections
we torture
              our grand finale
fireworks of pogroms
                         skeletons on fire

glory   glory
the executioner's peaceful face
the sweet hand that butchers
and the universe flows
                          with its run-of-the-mill moralities
again and again
the nectar of evil
the life-giving nature of suffering
skimmer diaphragms
                      ball of bulbs
glory
o the executioner's noble gaze
the background music of cyanide pills
o the emanation of this vitriol
we are waiting
corpses or fossils
and the macabre party
suddenly turns into an ordeal

we torture
and torment those who struggle
and bomb the rabblerousers
and sever that which ties

                              crimes on the table

glory   glory
we are the chosen people
standing
              on the tiptoes of destiny
for us the tomorrows that sing
the rivers of honey
                        and milk
sacrifice, brothers
                        sacrifice
exile in sacrifice
o the grand finale of throats
                              ready for the sacrifice
heritage
          Abraham's sadism
heritage
          faith struck down by miracles
the desert's spontaneous abundance
m i r a c l e
                    we don't suffer
o the hired killer's unblemished brow
the tickling of electrodes
and the scalpel that strips the vertebrae clean
again
      and again
breathe in all the gases
                        and greedily
                              swallow the grenades

glory
to the firing squad
kiss both the front
                and the back
of the trained finger
                  that caresses
                            the trigger
                                    that kills us

the spark melts
stillborn
having avoided the scalping
                        of the law
I didn't want to be a part of this theatre
no
puppet
        I didn't want to be executed
ludicrously
                on the bleachers
but to instead remain a valve
                        seaweed
a body beating with elemental breath
diastole
           to remain a pharynx
                        without
the possibility of a better life
I belong to this night
                    which doesn't dismantle the day
I'm not dough
             I'm yeast
to become at last a part of this poisonous tangle of roots

a flat-out refusal
the so-called problems of talking organisms
I reject
       this procreation of automatons
you have unpeopled languages
and the world
you have unpeopled
               life
forgotten the forgiveness
of stone
      of solidified
           mass
from one mass to another
              a clash
the stale air of shanties
              the hanging gardens
we're still dying
        of hunger
I'm not talking about war
about the recolonisation of the third world
about those transplants that didn't take
I alone rejoice
in these
      tortures
like a goatskin that is emptied
              into my flesh
                  the poem

I answer violence
         with violence
I won't control my fist's impulsiveness
patience
all these lives belong to me

I will talk about everything
before a hired assassin
                              comes to stab me in the back
patience
I'm going to speak
of the dead that went before me
both those I knew
                    and those yet to come
everything will be out in the open
this is my pledge to you
those dogs have stained our memory
who will want anything to do with this history
where slimy rats have scurried
one must destroy first to begin
then recidivism
the official accounts
                    w i l l   n o t   m e n t i o n   u s
napalm will gunk up the machine gun
the blowpipe shoots from the rear
                                        the moon is coming soon
the islands
            the prairies
and dump the lot
                    into a desert of salt-flats
some martians will come finish off the survivors

hideous uglinesses
in the severity of the days of retribution
I see nothing but killers
this brotherhood of killers
that bends the bow
the target thrown
                    inside the crime

hail barbarity of great famines
hail tribal arrowheads
hail jungles of barbarism
something in me reawakens
once again the miracle of the body
I begin by denying
my hand goes up
                    breaks
                        and then returns
to grab my genitals
                    cold and limp

Urgent Life

I remind chaos
of the rallying cry
                    d i s o b e d i e n c e
there will be wars
and sieges bloodier than the crusades
I want virtuous blood
                    rightful vengeance
Nobody consulted us before murdering us

raids
      uncertainty
                    stampedes
at every border
                    and scrub-land
why not us
            why not war
The War
            war at last
the rebellion of speech
but no tear-gas love stories
                            nor ecstasy pills
a major, all-consuming war
                            that exposes
                                    the pillory of fatalism
the journey cannot outpace the tick-tock
without a fixed rendezvous
a song cut short by vertigo of the bottomless chasm
the journey that stirs the world
                            into a savage denunciation

volcanoes start to rumble again
away with you
                        polygon of rebellion
the tree tied to my demented, refugee
roots
          the wretched of your lands
(my blood is extradited
                              away from me
                                        beyond the borders of what
                                                  is human

suffering suffering
                        amidst the panic of cities
suffering
          the ashes of war
suffering
          the heart that is pulverised
the world
          wants to reassure us
the world
          is calling for decency
this void
          this suffocating vacuum
this tampon of ether
                        that stops us breathing

a planet without fire
                        the power of glaciers
neither firedamp nor avalanches
                              nor this monsoon of locusts and
                                                  amber
the gold of all colours

               the sun solidified
all that
          and man the fossil
inescapably
               rodent-like matter
                         all the way to the sperm
I do not trust
the disintegration of the Eye
                         the division of the senses
this atrophy worries me
as though I'd failed a class

today some people erect purgatories atop earthquakes
caravan-masters of the absurd
today some people feel alone
                    lonely little demons
and they'll grow even more so
                         until the final shipwreck of breath

the Earth
          hangs from a noose
you can't keep up with my excreta
I light my cigarette
                    with your fujiyamas
monsoon of geysers
                    an invasion of epidemics
and so the words
                    stand on my threshold

I proclaim my ascent
blood swims upstream

                              to the top of the peaks
neither a tidal wave
                              nor a deluge
it swells
              galvanised in my orgasms
I won't grow any rivers or roads
only stars
enormous stars
                        alternative forms of life
I downplay the significance ↵
                    of the earth
                                        this car-wreck hurtling
                                                        towards oblivion
why should I limit myself to the margins
                                        this fragment
                                                  this beaten path

what a joke
                  these ballistic firecrackers
what a joke
                  these giant guard-dogs
the farce
              your explosions
                          your expansionism
                                        your interventions
your s t e p o n t h e g a s ! w a r

who told you I'm not a cannibal
barbarian
inside my eye
                  are vampiric nettles
oblong candlesticks

my teeth grow
                                fangs
the monster
                this brain tumour
the candle tips over
                                refraction sucks life
huge coccyx
                hairy my navel
one swamp leads me to another
(Atlantis came to me again in a dream
bearing honey cakes)
I know
                the certainties of the flesh
which geneses I witnessed
which apocalypses I survived
but strength
                stubborn strength
wings propel me
                                in the migrations of iguanas
who tells this coupling of glands
these tarsal bones
                ligaments
                                around this cartilage
are but the beginnings of my mutation
The certainty
                that other fluids converse in our blood
filtering
                other starry earthworms
but I need spaces
                storms of deserted areas
disembarkation of silences
to really focus
                on my caverns

*

t h e   b o d y

        the source

erection

     digestion of fire

the whole body

        inside the body

enough of it it leaves my body to pulverise cities

all shards

     all bludgeons

          all darts

m y   b o d y

light

no

not light

    (I don't like that word)

a beam

    that's right

        a volatile beam

the body is set in motion

and spurts the operative

          event

            in the building site of lives

kingdom desert

      desert kingdom

dwarf desert blood of naphtha   armed Desert forces and royalties

Desert   the taboo of space   Desert the concentric circle

Kiss the hand and take your share   O desert in your concentration-

camp exile

desert

    asphalt poured over our heads

*

desert put a stop to your waves of mirages   Desert wall   Syntax
of my madness   Desert I found your absurdity at the bottom
of a well   Desert don't forget me   Desert I curse you   Desert
I c a n d o w h a t I w r i t e Desert   lead-lined coffin
Desert   Sieve of my hatred   Desert of song and black Stone
Desert my second skin   it is ours
this desert
            this flying
                torpedo

these hidden horizons
                        are an impossible burden
hole
    of our masks
                        starry with bullets
name
        hung on prison bars
                            on powder kegs
of our dog-like faces
futile suns
                vegetative
face to face
                alone at last
in this community of land-grabbing
come on
let's murder one another
                            brothers
nothing before
                nothing after
a string of mousetraps
all this clandestine theatre
                        on the street

face to face
                 in these circuses of tears
a tree in a trance
                        twists its roots
impoverished by the foolishness of power
our lives are brief
                        towers of pebbles built on borders
that reassure us
Here we are, the first stage of our ruin
two millennia spurned
                              due to a miscalculation
by dictators masquerading as messiahs
and the spectre of fear is more catastrophic
                                    than megaton bombs

my desert
            I raise the finger
of the little countryside of the starving peoples
of the improvised charity field-hospitals
I feel like stuttering
                        with the audacity of a stammerer
from the depth of my entrails
s t o p   d e s e r t
                    banquet of ruins
stop
    stop
        this depopulation
and finally   w o r d
it was necessary this act
                        this abduction
at first I take
with the energy of a solid crowd
                        of a shiny new penny

do an about-face
                file for bankruptcy

o immemorial crime
if I arm myself to the teeth
                       it's to tear down the framework of dogmas
cannibal
      heap of glands
inseminating nausea
              under your masks

I see them again
              one by one
in one of those dreams where it seems right to forget
all the informers in the cafés
the whole tribe of the snow-sprinklers
there is no snow
no more quibbling over essences
no more fisticuffs in the straits
but the dissolution of man
the upside-down mouth
             of pain-farts
the horde of people who queue up
in front of the treacherous carrot
entertains
the dance has lost its smooth talkers
the oblivion when the prophet's companion circulated his dogmas
among those thirsting for eternal life
and not the conflagrations of signs
the tar that emerges out of your throat on a foggy morning

*

comrades
        we must remain alert
keep our distance
booed by everyone
              hands on the chest
and on the sidelines
              the newborn babies
learn therefore to read this epic of silence
                        in the alleyways

from one end to the other
                the blowing up
of salt balloons for future generations
and the horizon is kept under lock and key
                      by a tyrant's blacksmith
Caesar
        hand over the keys
Rome the eternal cannot burn again
my pen is deadly and I was told about the sighs of suicides on the
battlements where thistles are grazed on and I was told that the
roses are exiled to the caravan of undesirables

w h o   g a v e   m e   t h e   p o w e r   t o   d e c l a r e

stumble
        marked out paths
                one day at a time
cheap junk
a burning smell inside my brain
the panic
to return
        the pageantry of zulus

                              ennobled by scars
go back to hell
                    runaway escalation of mutations
I no longer
            find myths impenetrable

drum
      ululating females
I synchronise
                  the growing mosaic of cromlechs
cataract word
conveys my cunning
                        to the bedside of the world
the transfigured mountain
close your textbooks
                    jungles tortures
                                standardised
I never wrapped my head around your equations
if monkeys learned the language of eagles we'll pass a thousand
                                        suns through a sieve
may Africa forgive me
                    and the maghrebi trilogy
don't we have eyes
as centrifugal
                as lightening which strikes three times
as it is
      raw
            naked
                  effigies of your chatter
I must warn
          strike hard
                    and righteously
in order to inexorably

                    put wrongs
                                    to right

the story of the flood
springs out of the prophetess's tambourine
the signalmen dwarves in the sanctuaries
the Mahdi rises again
approach the cliff
                                and be hard as marble
avalanches avalanches
                                    dinosaurs among us
the disembowelled ark
                            more of the elect few
the prophetess
                    ochre hands
                                foamy hard-on
for crosses as they regain ground
the pupil in the seat of the world
watch over her epilepsy
                                she's raving in the forbidden tongue
I believe in the oracle of lost women
not on our side
'don't give up on the dream with which the mountain abounds'
rattlesnakes of murders
she said no
                to the kidnapping of the future
and her grave
                    grows larger among us

if our voices ever meet
                            it will be at the pitch of cries
don't we have hands

if our hands meet
                    it will be at the top of barricades
don't we have weapons
if we draw our weapons
                    it will be atop fences
don't we have bullseyes
there was a time when miracles were met by applause
the desert has understood
it has multiplied its numbers of hyenas
thrown out the idealistic camel-herders
I see the desert again
                    encroaching on my threshold
level with the walls
the donkey-drivers sell sand
                    water flows freely
the desert has no voice
                    no hands
                    no weapons
it feeds on Mistakes
                    and smuggles us
d e s t i t u t i o n

how can one speak
                    after the ravages of the desert
the prophetess forgets herself
a suckling infant
                    nursed by wind
tragedy in the vulture's talons
we watch lightning strike
                    we are sheltered
that the scales yield the verdict
196. 27 May 3:21 p.m. in Rabat
I can predict all future earthquakes
the mutual identification of victim and executioner

everybody up in arms when we longer know who gives and who
                                                        takes
some poets will never say enough
their voices should be the most monstrous drum imaginable
a kind of geodesic dome covering the entire planet
so that it stuns
                    every single
                                skull

yonder
grisly anthills spill their surplus of humanity
nothingness was
                    permanent shells
                                encase us
look at my fist
inhale the odour of death
(hate crimes
            or solar energy?)
do not tell me about the tribulations of instinct
I know my path
                    etched on the solstice
but what have we
                    what do we suffer from
rush so that I may watch
                    so I may paraphrase your mutism
hey cadavers
            I bet you've lost the power of speech

when
    vortex
        earth
            the predicted disaster

we'll no longer make head nor tail of it all
little cry of Nagasaki
little guerilla from the Caribbean
leave me now to write

                      the most dreadful of love songs

The Poem Beneath the Gag

(1981)

Chronicles from the Citadel of Exile

Write, write, never stop. Tonight, and for all nights to come.

When I finally found myself alone and had to take stock of the situation. Away with my uniform. I'm no longer like a lost land-surveyor wandering around a circumscribed area. I no longer obey those miserable orders. My prisoner number stays behind the door. I'm fed up with drinking, eating, urinating and defecating. I'm fed up with talking just to call things by their hackneyed names. I chain-smoke one cigarette after another, the smoke shoots out of my lungs in bursts and flies off in acrid plumes of denials. The prison-like night has swallowed up the artificial lights of day. Dishevelled stars populate the vault of my visions.

Write.

When I stop, my voice becomes very strange. As though obscure notes clung to my vocal chords, driven by unfamiliar storms, having come from all the lands where life and death look at one another and spy on one another, two uniquely-coloured beasts appear, both crouching down, ready to pounce, rip apart and destroy the underlying principle of the other.

Write.

I can only keep living by tearing myself away from myself, tearing out my stitches and my failures, there, where I feel closer to my heartbreaks, the collisions, there, where I de-fragment into pieces to live once more in countless elsewheres: earth, roots, spectacular trees, a grainy effervescence in the light of the sun.

Write.

When indifference disappears. When everything speaks to me. When the sea of my memory turns rough and its waves come crashing against the shore of my eyes.

I tear apart amnesia, and stand up, fully-armed, and become

the implacable reaper of what is happening to me in the light of what has already happened to me.

Easy does it, inner turmoil. Easy does it, my despair over what slipped through my fingers. Easy does it, my fury to live.

Write.

Even when it's impossible to simply think of you. And when my hand can no longer put up with burning due to your absence, your regular or anxious breaths, the smell of your hair, the end-lessness of your shoulder, that silence where I can feel every variation of your emotions flow through me. You move a hand, cross or uncross your legs, your eyes twitch and I know exactly what kind of shudder ran through you, the moment when that uncomfortable light bothers you, the moment when your nostrils flare at the birth of a new smell, the image, yes the sleek image that blurs your vision. Is so much happiness even possible? You have goosebumps only on your left arm and you plunge once again into that wave we share, which lulls us.

Easy does it, tenderness. Easy does it, my craving for certainties. Easy does it, my aphasia-destroying dream.

Write, write, and never stop.

Ten years? What does that amount to in the equation of life? It was a dawn, in the hollow palm of your warmth. When did you fall asleep? What time did I get back? Then the doorbell started ringing like crazy. They were knocking the door down with their fists. We understood right away. I leaped out of bed, went to stand by the window, and cautiously parted the curtains. The black car was parked down there on the street. Its headlights switched off. A Fiat 125. All our doubts evaporated. Then we started making all the necessary preparations, as though we were about to leave on a long journey. The doorbell rang like crazy. They were knocking the door down with their fists.

Write.

It would be impossible not to. I thought and thought until I fried my brain pondering this need that took a hold of me. Which has exercised its hold on me for so long. Which means that the reality which appears before me is always geared to another reality that is yet to come. Which means that the present is a constant project, the place where I accumulate matter, the building materials of an edifice which I don't know anything about for the time being, and which I can only comprehend as the pulsing of a new organ which had lodged itself in me, which has grown until it has started to hurt and gradually began to organise its activities. How could I describe this fanatical and watchful espionage of the real? And its arena is the vast theatre of our struggle, our suffering, our genocide and our revolutions, all the liveliness that buckles under the yoke of silence, under the weight of all those clandestine cries, all those decapitated memories.

I thought and thought until I fried my brain pondering this need that took a hold of me. Easy does it, clarity. Easy does it, my hostility against the darkness of the unspeakable.

Write.

A freezing January morning. The first day of exile. I was curled up on a bench, my hands and feet in chains. A rag covered my face entirely. Water dripped down and seeped through the cloth, spilling into my nose. It was impossible to drink it.

'Pour it in small quantities', I heard one man tell another.

'And you, keep his head leaning against the bench', the same voice whispered.

'Pour some more, just a little more', the voice continued, growing annoyed.

'That's enough now,' the voice concluded.

One would have thought it was some kind of practical demonstration around a dissection table. 'Professionalism', the desire to do a 'good' job.

I couldn't see them. I could hear their voices coming from varying distances, or the noise they made scraping their shoes along the ground. Greasy hands pinned my head against the bench. I was slowly suffocating. I thought about the rhythm of my resistance and my approaching death. Yet what image, what flurry of ideas could fully encapsulate the longness of that moment, while my lifeline slowly unravelled, thinning into a laundry line that is violently stretched when pulled at both ends, and which was nearing the point when all the threads would start to snap, one after the other?

Write, never stop.

Every page must triumph over this discomfort, this feeling of futility that paralyses me from time to time. One can only write, write if only to shake the authorities from their siege mentality, which has turned each road into a trap, when the torture shacks are full to capacity, when a people sees all its blood spilled on a daily basis, when a country's put up for auction, and cut up into big and little lots comprising brothels, murderous bases, flesh-grease for automobiles and slave hands. And to think that the average man on the street, that teenagers tossed out onto the streets of unemployment and aimlessness neither know nor recognise the deathly-pale face of that familiar unhappiness: waiting, police batons, disdain, bullets, hardened hatred.

Easy does it, torments of doubt. Easy does it, nausea. Easy does it, my irredentist volcano.

Write.

This night ahead of me, made brand new by its silence, by words that bloom, organise themselves and come weave themselves into my breath and turn it into a voice. It's good to smoke.

A train whistles in the distance. It's drawing near. A swarm of invisible fireflies. Heat in the train-cars. The bar filled with customers. Sleepy travellers tossing about in their dreams, which are more or less erotic.

A train-car detached itself, and rolled along the Andalusian plain, giving Granada back to me. The two of us in Granada. Everything was marvellous: leaning on a bar drinking a small glass of sherry, holding hands, spelling out the names of streets, watching the artisan calligraphers – the heirs of the Alhambra's traditions – practise their art, asking for directions from people walking by, and even our most basic conversations with them filled us with the thrill of human camaraderie, then going to sleep and waking up with the same intensity. Granada, where loving one another was devastating.

A train whistles in the distance. It's drawing near. It goes right through me. It exits the tunnel of my body. And once again, the silence that seems to only slightly bother the timid barking of a dog, who was probably stirred from his sleep by the noise.

Write.

Day by day, the noose tightens. Prisoner! What is there to say? A typical cell *par excellence*: approximately eight-by-five feet. Minimum cubic standards, it seems. A light bulb that oozes misery thanks to its twenty-five watts, which is encased in the wall, placed beyond reach by a massive pane of frosted glass, a squat toilet topped with a copper faucet, the small regulation window with suitably thick bars (also regulation), and – a great luxury – a shelf where the 'lodger' can arrange his belongings. In front of you is the grey door with its judas hole, which is also obscured by an ingenious mechanism consisting of a sliding metal bar, which in its turn was perfected by another security feature involving a piece of iron wire that runs through a ring situated in the middle of the bar and is securely attached to its base. Finally, you've got the cement platform covered in plaster, which pompously takes up half the available space and is where the mattress is situated. This is where the lodger holds court atop his throne, sleeps, has nightmares, and sometimes, having reached the end of a labyrinth of dark thoughts and hallucinations, decides to commit suicide. Naturally, we are in the 'Central House', the crown jewel of prisons in this sunny country.

Write.

Day by day, the noose tightens. Day by day, it loosens. The surreal, silent sky comes alive when it is filled with a swarm of nimble clouds, reproducing the earth's gesture. The sun leaps over the walls, turning the tables on the greyness and reassuring all in sight that spring is on its way. Air circulates, bloated by inextricable messages. Unstoppable birds spread their coloured wings, build, reproduce, learn to steal, keep their eyes pinned on the shiny mirrors, reflecting the parade of life. The dream swells, becoming an organic vision of what clarity has revealed. There are no certainties for the future, it saturates the present with its materiality.

Day by day, this miracle which consists in living, changing, learning to love one another better, nourishing stronger hopes, experiencing happiness, doing away with solitude, marching to the beat of the world's heart, in the very heart of a citadel erected to ensure a slow death, humiliation, sheep-like submission, cynicism, savage sadness, human exile.

Write, write, and never stop.

The itinerary of our metamorphosis. Which one of us converted the other to the requirements of love? How could I possibly sort through this undivided patrimony to figure out which dazzling gifts you brought me, or know the fiery gifts I placed in your hands? What is love built on, what is it that constantly transfigures it? And what makes it tragic, turns into a blind, selfish wall? What breaks it when it flows like all the unconscious streams of existence and what leads it to rise from the ashes and the worn pelts of old men and women?

There are so many areas of man that need to be regenerated, while there are many windows left to open in his heart, so many faculties that could be freed from the cave in which they're hibernating. Once those old illusions have been destroyed, the real difficulty will lie in not creating any new illusions to take their place. Because love is a fragile continent, which is always emerging, a continent illuminated by the sun which we always disembark on. And if we know the odyssey that led us there, we have so much left to explore, and so many other adventures await us.

Write.

Is this the only trial that made us into what we became, in our reciprocal relationship, or our relationships with other people? We had to get to know one another, hurt one another, going from stomping our feet in anger, to stammering, shutting up, isolating ourselves because we felt misunderstood, happily triumphing when a ray of light came to bring us new meanings of tenderness, embracing our aimlessness, opening up a new path for us so we could reach an unprecedented milestone. Then we started to talk, while the world around us grew more real, and poetry humanised us, as our people fought and sacrificed themselves to allow us to have a homeland we could actually live in, and finally while we woke up to this gift. This was our odyssey, at the end of which we discovered that our hands looked incredibly similar, and discovered our human camaraderie.

Write.

Once again, an immeasurable night. A plane suddenly bursts out of the silence. Its rumble explodes as though something had gone wrong with the plane's organs. It must prepare to land. Why is this all so agonizing? My body's like a resonating chamber that tingles from head to toe. You see, a mere nothing triggers your presence in me, which cannot limit itself to being a mere memory, but instead convulses me while I lie on the bed, clenches my throat, makes me put my pen down, mechanically light a cigarette and takes me far away from this bar-crossed place which defies the passing of time and to somewhere where you and I can walk together side by side, happy.

Write.

I must confess this. I have some confidence in the power of words, even though I move them around in any way possible, even if I speak them out loud to ensure that their timbre hasn't been ruined, and that a lower-quality word hasn't snuck its way into their flock. And when I line them up and arrange them, I have to read them and re-read them, in order to ensure that what I've written isn't esoteric or estranged from what I think of as acceptable, such as our common suffering and our common hopes. Writing entails this responsibility. And starting from the moment where I take up those responsibilities – oh yes, I did just that – it becomes impossible to beat around the bush or to content yourself with approximations. One must be able to defend every word, every sentence, and if you've got nothing to defend, to ensure that they target the sensibilities of each and every one of us, until they become as familiar to our ears as the crackling rain, which is indispensable to the earth, like the innumerable – and often strange – flowers without which spring cannot come into its own.

Yet, easy does it, intransigence. Easy does it, rational demon of poetry.

Write, write, and never stop. Tonight, and for all nights to come.

Yet another night when it's impossible to do anything but write, jostling against this silence that challenges me through the idiom of exile. At best, I try to explore this voice of the prison-like night. I listen, and little by little grow to understand its harmony, I move along its surface and receive its bloody echoes. I hunt the silence down and usurp its powerful voice, while its damns start to buckle more and more, collapsing in a roar which amazes me, which scatters away into the night.

The country comes to me, an aerial chant that surged out of the depths of history, a crucible of incandescent sparks and sweat, of oiled muscles that hammer down on the anvil of rebellious matter, of planting seasons, harvests, of bread and black olives shared out amongst people, the froth that boiling tea makes in the glass, which is passed from hand to hand, trumpets, accordions and drums prompting the streets into colourful processions, laughter and rambunctious children drunk on music and fragrances, the reddish ankles of women perched on round tables beating time with their feet, vibrant breasts like fresh, ripe pomegranates, a frenzy of rattlesnakes, musicians playing off-key who ostentatiously slay overheated violins, electrocuted tambourines, disembowelling plump string instruments, showing off the range of their scales.

A long silence then the country comes back to me, with a devastated face, which is completely unrecognisable. Screams here or there, a fight, a rape, a murder. The cries of wild-eyed children who are flogged so that they learn to keep their mouths shut. Mourning cries and women in tears who scratch their cheeks with their fingernails, tearing out their hair, lashing the ground with their scarves, punching their thighs, and beating their heads against walls. The cries of babies left abandoned in shantytown shacks, in the penumbra of neediness. Cries sparked by malnutrition and illness. Cries unleashed by women beaten half to death by desperate, drunken men. The groans and gaps of those terrified women, who kiss the feet of their aggressors to beg for

mercy, for God's mercy, for their children, for their shared mis-
ery. The cries carried by the odious winds of March's insurgency,
when students were gunned down in the middle of the day by a
false, traitorous Independence, armoured dinosaurs crushing tiny
dreams hatched in the heat of the day and the smiles of men. The
cries of my comrades tied to torture trestles and *pau de araras*, or
even *parillas*. The cries when the cry becomes the Esperanto of
resistance, the slow epic of hope and human drama. Oh, my dear
comrades, my flesh is hallucinating, and my heart is so full of love
that it can't stand it any more, your eyes, which are so unforget-
tably full of promises, our irrepressible tenderness.

Write.

While standing halfway through my journey, with my neck in
a noose and after many wounds, I write.

The galloping
                    years pass by
The scissor-dials destroy the clock-face
crushing the hand of the Cyclops
                              as he sits slumped on his
                                                    throne
and my people march on
and I continue to exist
                    a rebel

Prison Cell

I never wanted to talk about you
prison cell
you're so banal
                    and so bleakly familiar
like the noose they lift and let fall
with every step that we take
but the problem, prison cell,
is that today
you force yourself on me;
your craters of chalk
spring to life like a carnival's bestiary,
your hopeless door
with that sniggering jaw through the peep-hole
your window unto a hypothetical sky
that calls out to nostalgias
You're right here
inside me
like a second body
that pushes me deeper and wanders through me
after blowing the cold wind
of exile into my chest
and I'm not ashamed
of being a little down in the dumps today
in this clandestine display case of separation
I'm not ashamed to feel my fuming broken heart
tumble inside me
the unmistakeable tragedy
that keeps running alongside me
the happiness of final certainties

Death

Here I am, thirty-three
and I too start to think
about death
I'm not talking
about death with a capital D
but simply my own
which might arrive any day now
and is an experience with which
I must settle some scores
These aren't bleak ideas
or a case of 'existential angst'
no
since I must be in prison for many years
where each day and each night
comes courtesy of my torturers
this is just me being realistic

Death of mine
I want you to be sweet like those happy dreams
where despite all the obstacles
I reach the end of the maze
and catch and stroke my beloved wife's hand
remembering the real colour of her eyes
feeling the petal-like tear
form in the torch of her pupil
Sweet is how I want you
a single image
that sums the splendour of the human onslaught
all the promises offered by life
I want you to be

like a quivering ray of dawn–light
a forest of hands that carpets the planet
and warm laughter and furious drums
and flutes that banish the same old solitudes

You'll be free to tap me on the shoulder then
death of mine
and I'll follow you without a trace of reluctance
I won't leave behind me
either a hidden treasure
or any real estate
merely a few words
for the second coming of man
and this miraculous tenderness
that allows me
death of mine
to defy your mechanical stare
and slip into a peaceful sleep
knowing that my dreams
won't crumble into dust
like my husk of a body,
but will bloom on the paths
that men will walk down on
while exchanging their views
and embracing
and continuing the struggle

The Stroll

This morning
after a long time in the hole
they let me out
for a fifteen-minute walk
into an empty corridor
littered with rusty cans
and bits of broken glass
An 'official' stood guard at the gate
while another
stood at the other side of the track
with a rifle on his back
All this for the sake
of a sick man
weakened by two weeks of hunger strikes
Yet being looked at like an animal
as though I were some wild beast
whose each harmless gesture should be suspect
doesn't affect me any more
I even know that those men
who watch my every step
might even sympathise with me
or might at least be indifferent
because they too were hungry and miserable
There was a crazy-bright sun
and the sky was blue, so blue that when I looked up at it
I didn't know where to turn my head
So I shut my eyes
and bathed my hands and face
in that unsettling marriage of elements
then my heart resumed

its natural rhythm
the regular beat of hope

Hunger Strike

Let's talk about this hunger strike
It's a form of resistance
that men in my situation
have experimented with throughout the long history
of mutilations
Sure it's a passive act
but when you've got nothing but your naked chest
against Fascist arsenals
the only weapon we've left
is this irrepressible
breath still inside us
which we push to the furthest of limits
risking its death
to safeguard our dignity

When you're hungry
the sun looks bleached
and the sleepless nights are freezing
We think about so many
weighty or funny things
When I was less serious I admit
I was tormented by the idea of earthly delights
I imagined such a bunch of tasty treats I could eat
that I ran through the gamut of my gastronomical knowledge
but there we have it, I'm not ashamed of such thoughts
because what prevails
during this wait
this journey towards the unknown
is the feeling of immense strength
at the heart of weakness

how he who resists is superior
to he who oppresses
Yes life is a formidable weapon
that will always frighten
the armies of cadavers
Once again what prevails
is the brotherhood of sufferings
What tortures the hungry
is this vile putrid taste in the mouth
those cold bulging eyes in the fog of the day
the despairing emptiness
that makes the gut clench and twist
Once again what prevails
is the brotherhood of sufferings
The ideas that cut through the night
become tangible things
they belong neither to me
nor the other, nor to another still
but are the property
of all those excluded from the light of the sun
Once again what prevails
is the brotherhood of sufferings
because our hunger
isn't conjured by mirages of El Dorados
isn't the lust for supercities that kneel
before the golden calf and debauchery
our hunger belongs to a new world
peopled by new men
to a sun that is shared
without thought of profit
to an irreversible sense of peace
to the chagrin of the builders of inequality
Furthermore
during these days of abstinence

it makes me proud
that going hungry
means I get to unsettle
the perverse complacency
of those who starve my people

The Policeman's Speech

He stared me down
His gaze seemed to scan for some object
somewhere behind my back
to my right
amidst the heap of dirty rags
lying at my feet
somewhere under my soles
He talked and he talked and he talked
for his sake
for the sake of the walls
for the sake of a public
of dull, bleating sheep
He talked and he talked and he talked
while he digested his lunch
to kill some time
to thwart the sun filtering through
despite the black ring surrounding the city
He talked and he talked and he talked
showing off all his know-how with his fists
and the handcuffs that dangled from his belt
like an emblem of power
– 'Solidarity, self-defence!
What a meaningless
                    pile of shit!
It's none of your business
Solidarity
          it's in your interest
to seek solidarity with yourself, your children, your family
it's every man for himself out there
you need to be crafty

how to go about furthering
your interests, and yours alone!'
– '...'
– 'Socialism you say
It'll never catch on with Arabs
Let's talk about Russia
over there, they got women climbing ladders
and carrying sacks of cement on their backs
women – do you understand what I'm saying
is that what you call socialism?
Do you know that our kids who go study in Russia
take pairs of blue jeans and shoes with them
because people pay top dollar for them?
Is that the future you want for us?'
– '...'
– 'And what about China, eh?
You admire the Chinese, don't you?
So where's Lin Biao
who was the first to wave the *Little Red Book* about
why did he run away
unless he actually realised
his country was headed for ruin?'
– '...'
– 'If only people listened to me
I'd round up all the Reds and slit their throats
We can get along with pretty much everyone
even Republicans
but not the Reds'
– '...'
– 'Socialism you say
but who's really a socialist in the Middle East?
Only those penniless,
flea-ridden Yemenis
but as for us, thank God,

we want for nothing
and everyone's got enough to eat
Unemployment? Nothing but bullshit
it's just slackers who dodge honest work
choosing instead to be drug dealers and thieves'
– '…'
– 'Socialism, communism
it's just one black hole after another
that's all, they're just ideas
and ideas evolve
they're like mountains that never meet
Solidarity, self-defence
seek solidarity with yourself
it's every man for himself out there
and look after your own interests!'
He talked and he talked and he talked
hurling his words against the wall of my silence
and that voice
with its repulsive stench of opportunism
which stank like the latrines of the Old World
flew right over my head
and got lost
somewhere behind my back
to my right
amidst the pile of dirty rags
lying at my feet
somewhere under my soles

Four Years

Soon enough it will have been four years
since I tethered myself to you
to my comrades
to my people
they chained me up
gagged me
blindfolded me
banned my poems
banned even my name
exiled me to a little island
of rust and cement
and painted a number
on my back
they forbade me
the books that I love
novels
music
and in order to see you
for fifteen minutes a week
through two grills separated by a hallway
they had to be there
drinking the blood of our words
with stopwatches inside their heads
instead of brains

Freedom

It's been a while now since I started
being viciously snapped
out of my daydreams
then looking around myself
and wondering
What am I doing here
am I really in prison?
A strange feeling
that lasts for a moment
when you feel the irrepressible impulse
to put your freedom to use
that very instant
whereas your real situation
strangles you
overwhelms you
with the weight of its evidence
the hand that bore the gift
and your gesture falls
your freedom emigrates
towards other dreams
which begin to acquire
a slightly savage taste
and irredentist shapes
These multiply
whirling so madly
around your failed dream-act
transforming into the eye of a whirlwind
that spins and spins
until you digest it
so as to nourish

all the possibilities
all that can't be destroyed
what once stirred and nourished
all of humanity's needs
all that once
broke through the stranglehold

To My Son Yacine

My beloved son,
I received your letter
where you spoke to me like an adult
told me all about how hard you studied at school
and where I saw that your passion for learning
chased all the darkness and ugliness away
as you delved into the secrets of the big book of life
you're confident
and you rattle off your pearls of wisdom
with the greatest of ease
you reassure me by telling me how strong you are
as though you wanted to tell me: 'Don't worry about me
look how I can walk,
look at where my steps take me,
the horizon, the huge horizon over there
holds no secrets for me'
And I picture you
with your beautiful
straight brow
I picture how proud you are

My beloved son,
I received your letter
where you said:
'I think about you
and I make you a gift of my life'
you will never know
what an effect you had on me by saying that
the effect you had on me by saying that
my crazy heart

my head among the stars
and thanks to your words
it's no longer difficult to believe
that the Big Feast will soon arrive
the one in which children like you
who once they will become men
will take giant steps
far from the miseries of the shantytowns
far from hunger, ignorance and poverty

My beloved son,
I received your letter
you wrote the address all by yourself
spelled it out confidently
told yourself, if I do this
then daddy will get my letter
and maybe I'll get a reply
and you started picturing prison
the big house where people are locked up
who knows for how long and for what reason?
But this means they cannot look out on the sea
or the forest
and this means they're unable to work
so they can feed their children
You imagine something bad
not nice
something that doesn't make any sense
which makes you feel sad
angry beyond belief
Also you think
that the people who built prisons
must have been crazy
and many other thoughts like that
Yes, my beloved son,

this is how we start to reflect
to understand human beings
to love life
to hate tyrants
and all this explains how and why
I love you
love to think about you
from the abyss of my prison

Letter to My Friends Overseas

Friends
you've become
one of those beacons of light
who help to defend me
from the forceps of the night
You find your way to me
through the mercy of the poem
and I'll see you again
beyond the barbed wire of exile
in a stillborn continent
that never surges out of the sea or the sky
nor is fashioned out of clay
but by the hands and the fervour
of voices that plead and jump out of the window
to plunge into the swell of possibilities
A human continent
that nurses the preamble
of all the sleeping or reawakening gifts
inside us all
which despite the hurdles of baseness
work their way through our flesh
and our consciences
A continent
where suspicion, contempt and indifference to the other
one day will look
like poorly-written plays
and be entombed in the mass grave
of obsolete currencies
A continent
where the Inquisition
will vanish from our brains

after this kingdom of barbarism crumbles
where intelligence
will fuse with feeling
where conversations without masks
will be welcomed and peppered with peaceful greetings

Kind friends
usually when I write
I barely have the time
to feel your warmth
and sit amongst you
(a cigarette in my lips, the same tune in my head)
and must leave you
before I've reached the end of the page
You see, here they ration out
even the stationery
The request forms I fill
only allow correspondence
between the prisoner
and his family
They'll never understand
that family to me
doesn't mean ancestry
or heredity
or villages or ID cards
I've never been able to estimate
the size of my family
It stretches out
as far the sunrise in our eyes
as far as our newly-born continent
tears down the walls erected inside us

Friends
I've got so much to tell you:

it's just that usually
I keep my mouth shut not wanting to risk
the censors putting a stop
to these acts of presence
in fact I censor myself
fearing the briefness of my answers
might twist my thoughts
out of shape for you
or warp what this humble letter
this gradual rediscovery of ourselves
these simultaneously peaceful upsetting accounts
of the other through dialogue
have to say

Friends
I grow more convinced
that the poem
can only ever be
a dialogue
made of live flesh and sound
that stares you straight in the eyes
even if the poem has to cross
the cold wastes of distance
to finally reach you
in the creases created by absence
This is why
you no longer hear me speaking alone
in the trances of exorcism
in my tragic haemorrhages
as I extricate myself from this quagmire
and call out to the earthquake survivors
to heap my distress calls and curses on them
A long time ago
I wrote those poems

about the infernos of solitude
about my desperate climb back to my fellow human beings
and I'm not quite ready to disown them
those bitter fruits
of the murderous twilight
where I struggled
as I sought the roots
of a voice I knew was my own
of a human face that reflected
the exact image of my truth
Those violent poems were healthy
and without them
maybe my voice
today would be hollow
devoid of what gave it
its vital intensity
But the problem is
I can't write like that any more
Nowadays
my life's taken a different path
and so has my style
I'm not alone any more
My ordeal has placed me
on the road of encounters
My body has learned
to be pushed to the limits and curl up
as from a scalding-hot steel plate
to endure the lacerations
and to resist
to translate humiliation and pain
into their literal opposites
and inside this lead-sealed arena
where they condemned me to shuffle
for ten whole years

I have started to dig
entire tunnels
and underground passages
even into my veins
even into my mind's vital parts
and I heard other people were digging
in all the directions towards which
I was piercing through my aphasia
until the day when the first hand broke through
and I felt the willowy vines of embraces

Friends
you've often asked yourselves
how I got to this point
how a poet
can descend from his clouds
to walk on the earth
and turn into a warrior
Well here it is
you know my love
for my country and countrymen
and you can grasp
how in our stormy part of the world
these words are saturated with meaning
so that they can resonate
                              struggle
                                        and perish
for what they stand for
Your compassion for me
is glaring proof of that
Yes
if I'm here
it's because my passion was all-devouring
It destroyed my vague cravings for comfort

all the perks that being an intellectual
might have conferred upon me
all the illusions of cool-headed analysis
of the academic laboratories
There was no middle ground
It was either the gilded cage
of intellectuals-for-hire
an ostensibly servile
face-saving exercise,
or the brio of talent
that never accounts
for all the defeats and abuses
So I severed the moorings
and made for the wide-open sea
of the only struggle that matters
which my people are waging
and I can sing
out of love for this haunting land
this hijacked country
that electrocutes my memory
which serrates my distress
and hits me like a meteorite
magnetising the bend of its rainbows
unwinding its arabesques
revealing itself
as the gleaming giant of youth
who reaps the solar apotheosis
with a sphinx's dreamers' eyes
as it paws the ground inquisitively
a poppy pressed
to every artery torn from the body of life
so that blood abolishes
the winter of man

I can sing
out of love for this haunted land
which has turned into a poker chip
in the stock market of lawlessness
free it from the lies of slave-driver travelling salesmen
the clicking prayer-beads of billboards
in the stations of the West
where its sun
is a whorehouse for the pimps of bride abductions
where its veils and tattoos
are the opium of mystery
behind which the ghosts gasp for air and salivate
where the dignified faces of its men
are assaulted by old Kodak cameras and savage disorientations
O to what extent we stunt
and debase
        life!

I can sing
out of love for this haunted land
as it bleeds standing up
so its name resonates
like these warning-bell words
that reverberate in the heavens
of courage and brotherhood
so that they swell
out of these cutting-edge wounds
sing of the blood
of those who perished at the dawn of great hopes
so their names grow in stature
and each of their syllables
becomes as familiar
to the uprising of consciences
as Vietnam and Palestine

Friends
You who live in the sterilised labyrinths
of the fortress of Wealth
You who see the caravans of taxed swag
amassed by your Knights-Templar Merchants
from the pillaged realms of the world
as they pass under your windows
You the conscientious objectors
in the twilight between the wolves and dogs
where they scheme, interfere and exterminate
on every horizon
all for the sake of your supposed security
of your interests
of your existential outlook on life
You the gentle gardeners
of the tree of fraternity
before whose eyes
they still whisper
o so discreetly
while putting a gun, a knife and a grenade
into the filthy hands
of gallows-birds and nigger-wogs
while camouflaged under cover of fog
You who go hungry
because the sight of your roads
saturated with the rubbish of waste
makes you heave
You the entombed
banned from the old-boy networks
where they pre-package popular culture
and put it into little golden sachets
of mimicry and of ruins
You the motionless

the killjoys
in the prison-factories
the penny-jars
the temples of shopping
the plantation-colonies of the supercities
that enrich the inner sanctums of multinationals
decorated with the emblem of the golden calf
You the troglodytes
of black-magic spell-books where they whisper the universal
sound investments of the old missionary West
the belly-button of the world

All this and more
dear friends
you the harbingers
who've thrown open the windows
of your hearts and your hands
You who've dug up the beach
and the red, vivid sea of multitude
from under the cobblestones
You the new bards
of the street who
sing Communard songs
and flock back to the vigilant barricades
You thanks to whom
the West will one day disappear
from our legitimate nightmares
like the spectre of dispossession
like the jungle machetes
suspended right over our heads
You the artisans
who will repopulate Europe
and restore

its cities of marvels
and plant the seeds
for the springtime of humanity

O friends
be brave
for your sake and ours
be brave
wherever the tunnel of the night
seems like a dead end
be brave
We'll deflect the sun
to shine on our imperative journey
We'll disembark
in that new continent
that'll arise all over the world
whose seas
won't be private pleasure-lakes for bankers
or criss-crossed by aircraft carriers of carnage anymore
but instead become oceans
streaked with bridges
traversed only
by sailing boats of discovery
and convoys bearing gifts

Friends,
I'll stop here for now,
I don't know
if what I've written you
is a poem
and whether people
recognise it as such
doesn't bother me much
because poetry

to me
isn't an attitude one adopts towards language
or friezes of hieroglyphs
that we should decipher
aided by scholarly
parameters of criticism
Poetry spills out of the page
evades these insignificant labels
employed to confine it
                    pigeon-hole it
                              make it niche

Poetry to me
is simply a way
to hold out my hand
to push myself further
to rear my head again
                    and provoke
to herald all the brotherly suns

Kind friends
I'm so happy we've talked
Rest assured
my cell is far brighter
I feel like singing and laughing
and want to raise my glass
to our loves and hopes
What I've told you
doesn't add up to much
but our dialogue
has barely begun
and we've got a whole world to change
Adelante!

Editor's Note: The original text of 'Letter to My Friends Overseas' was first published in *La Nouvelle Critique* in August 1978, after being mailed out piecemeal to friends of Laâbi's in France and later assembled according to the poet's instructions. A truncated and transliterated English version appeared in *Index on Censorship* in 1980, in order to bring attention to Laâbi's worsening medical condition, by which time he had served seven years of his decade-long sentence.

The World's Embrace

(1993)

Crumblings

Look, my love,
at this world that is crumbling
around us
within us
Hold my head tightly against your chest
and tell me what you see
Why are you so silent?
Just tell me what you see
The contaminated stars fall
from the tree of knowledge
Will the toxic cloud of ideas
soon overwhelm us?

Tell me what you see
Are the books burning in the public squares
Are they shaving women's heads before stoning them to death
Are there processions of men in balaclavas
brandishing crosses and scimitars
Why are you so silent, my love,
are we standing on a floating island
or slicing through waves astride a torpedo
Are we alone
or are we chained to our brothers-in-suffering
What day is it
What time is it?

Hold my head tightly against your chest
and if you can
open your belly up and welcome me
into the crucible of your strength

Send me upriver
to the spring of all springs
Plunge me into the rock pool of life
and pour seven fistfuls of barley
on my head
while humming that song by Fayrouz
the one you can sing so much better than she can

Why are you crying
Are you worried about the world
or about our love
Is there nothing you can do for me?
So just tell me what you see
What evils are people dying of these days
What is this invisible weapon that is sucking
the unmistakable taste and soul of life
What is this caravan that devours its own camels
and empties its goatskins of water onto the sand
Who is this magician
who has turned war into an act of love?

Why are you so silent
Are you among those who believe that words are so dirty
that one can't even use them to ask for directions
Do you think there's nothing left to say
and that my poor little poems
only make a mockery of mockery
Would you prefer I kept my mouth shut
and let you look on as things fall apart
amidst the dignity of your silence?

Hold my head tightly against your chest
and cradle me
My head will become tiny

in the silly cocoon of your hands
The large abscess of ideas will burst
and I will re-become the child of another century
frightened by thunder
who steels himself
reeling off an old alphabet
by the light of a candle
in the forbidden house of Fez
next to a brazier where incense and fenugreek burn
and the evil eye exploded in the alum
Cradle this toddler whom nobody ever cradled
so he can come back to life and in your arms revivify
a drowned, pillaged world
of which nothing remains
except the bitter perfume of innocence

Why are you so silent, my love,
Did I re-awaken the pain you'd stifled
or perhaps the desire to be cradled yourself
The desires of a girl who was born in a different war
who travelled across those seas
to find the sun in her picture books once again
and caress the golden fruit in an orchard
guarded by legionnaires?
You ignored this vain torment of roots
which man loves more than his own voice
and quickly learned to speak the despised tongues
that know how to sow seeds in the lands where blood is spilled
and how to plant where deracination is dogged
All this while pretending to fly
with the loyalty of migratory birds
and this melancholy that sweetly lacerates them
between the nest and the journey

Why are you crying
Are you mourning this drowned world
or this crumbling world
Do you weep for children or adults
Can we choose between two kinds of goodbyes
resolve ourselves to farewells
even though the miracle is right here
in our peaceful heartbeats
which play their symphony
wrist against wrist
even if weapons are allowed to speak
instead of poets?

Hold my head tightly against your chest
and tell me what you see
with that careful eye we so patiently trained
in the darkest of darknesses
when we kept track of days by counting them backwards
when the spring devoured sex
when the autumn was a swallow made out of wax
on our pillow
when the summer seared our skin with its red-hot pokers
and the winter granted us a crumb of mercy
When some loving words hurled through the grills
kept us nourished for a whole, interminably long week
When I smiled at the conquest of your smile
and you spilled the tears I refused to spill
When I pulled a pigeon out of my head
so you could perch it proudly on your shoulder
while you lingered in the waiting line

Tell me what you see
with that fleshy, steely eye
that's so accustomed to the darknesses

old as time itself
the incontrovertible witness
Why are you so silent, my love,
this eye will never be extinguished, will it?
So tell me what you see
Have they started destroying Granada
Are the barbarians at our gates
What are the barbarians like
Do they speak a strange language
Do they really hail from another galaxy
from another temporal dimension
How do they resemble us
What about them is so terrifying?

Tell me what you see
Does the river of images still flow
Has a date been set for the Flood
Fighting's already broken out around the Ark
What will they do with wounded horses
with children no longer able to walk
Women have picked up weapons in their turn
Is there a lost prophet amidst the hordes?

Why are you so silent, my love,
You force me to imagine
what I've never wanted to imagine
even if it meant scooping out my own eyes
How could I have believed that one day I would have to take on
the crow's accursed job
or even the swan's sombre role
An artisan's son, I am now an artisan,
a weaver of hope
a keeper of the fireplace until it crumbles to ashes
a shepherd without a shepherd's crook

which I raise against the wolf-dog
An artisan's son, I am now an artisan,
who keeps only a single eye fixed on rainbows
to avoid confusing the colours
placing my trust in their names
picking them up one by one
and placing them inside my mother's copper pot
like all the other rare spices
destined for human pleasures
destined for a meal that only becomes lawful
when the poor bless and honour it

How could I have known
that the dream that led me to believe in humankind
would become a nightmare
that the heroes of my youth
would cut down the tree of my song
that the books where I met my doppelgängers
would turn yellow at the bottom of my shelves
that my roving, devoted to the encounter,
would leave me without a glass of water
or a piece of bread, left on the side of the road
by Whoever keeps watch over those who wander?

How could I have believed
in the mirage of such a beautiful road
in the chains of such a crazy horizon
in worms residing inside such beautiful fruit
Where can one thus find the flaw?

Why are you so silent, my love,
do you wish to fan the flames of words in me
make me blurt out pompous predictions, heresies
to remake with words what man

has destroyed with words
restore meaning to what has allied itself against meaning
bring the cogs and gears that have swallowed my body with a cry
leaving me nothing but the semblance of a voice
Yet who speaks within me
Is it you, or my eye,
or even my words which are in mourning
Go, therefore, word
relieve me
spin me into delirium
restore to my tongue its forgotten languages
its ancient beliefs
the restless hornets of its words
its jungles and its cool-headed reducers
Slip me from the noose of reason
Take my wolfskin and sheepskin
my fossilised inkwell, my pencils
the funerary bread on which I swore an oath
Take this pilgrim's staff
that thought it could lead a blind man
Take the last cigarette and throw away the packet

Go, my words
relieve me
spin me into delirium
be vigorous, abrasive, irritating
Rise up and overflow
Stand on your head
Wash the words dragged through the mud
and all those putrid mouths
Become a wave that swells
and inexplicably leaps out of the sea
along with all the fish who reject the destiny of water
Ensure another magma forms in you

a hardened lemon
and ensure it promises us an obstinate genesis
with neither heaven nor hell
as slow as the caress that stokes the flames of desire

Go, word,
my loyal words
Now I speak
with my whole body
with all my failures
Defeated, I refuse to give up
I'm going to open a building site in my memory
and light torches with the light of my martyrs' eyes
and use their hands to beat on drums
We're going to dance the dance
of suns that stole
butchered bulls from us
and threw them into our prison cells
where sacred dancers were imprisoned for the crime of dancing

O, words
Leave no organ fallow
water them with a youthful, pregnant juice
Dance with me
Dance with us
Whether there are ruins or no ruins
chaos or paradise
Whether God is dead or alive
Dance with everything
I come to you
poor and naked as I should
with a fistful of salt in my mouth
my nails long and blackened
walking on glowing coals

in a cloud of sandalwood smoke and fuming entrails
flying the black-and-yellow flag of crazed women
the priestesses of holes in the earth
I come to you
O mother and father
to join the procession and wear the robe
to link my faith to the rope of your faith
I've brought a billygoat and coloured candles from Salé
three sugar loaves
and a bundle of mint from Meknès
O, make room for me
so I can dance
and my blood can spurt onto the pavement
to show the path to the sanctuary
where no Imam can hide
This sanctuary which even you have forgotten
There where rebels escape human laws
and can live like free men
O, my words
dance with me
dance with us
I entrust this body to you in its healthy trance
its benign and malign tumours
these talismans encrusted in the skin
to instil the patience of stone
and make one's fate less voracious
I entrust you with
this procession which hesitates between frenzy and submission
I entrust you with
these drums, rattles
and seductive violins
I entrust you with
kettles and pitchers
the cauldron, the fire and its servants

I entrust you with
the virgin and the spirits who dwell in her
her polyphonic cry of false pregnancy
her blinding breasts
her hips which slice through the night like a winged ship
O, my unpredictable mistress
I entrust you with
the floodgates of the night
so that you can spring them open
at the appointed hour
without giving in
to the abductors of the dawn   .

O my words
where have I come from if not from you
and where am I going?
Now I've got nothing left except this hair
to bring me from one precipice to the next
and rejoin some friendly star
that stubbornly shines through the desolation of the sky
rise through the circles of an incoherent inferno
where some thought I would enjoy myself
Now I've got nothing except this kingdom
which is the size of a hand-span
where I don't even have a right to a tent
and where I can't even hear a name
without hurting
there where no suture can stitch the wound shut
Must I call you my homeland
to console me or to wreak my vengeance
or must I also let you be
free to rule over roots, heresies, love
forever rebellious?

O, Word
a force to be reckoned with
you alone can banish me
when no other tyrant can exile me
You alone can saddle my horse
or choose the bridle and stirrup
and lead it down frightening paths
where you enjoy yourself by making me read like a neophyte
through sand, pebbles and cold trails
You alone, o jealous woman,
can't condone either weaknesses or infidelity
And now you toss me aside like a soiled tissue
into this chaos
And now you assign me
the end of the world
and task me with sifting through the ruins
to discover the black or white stone
the missing seed
the ring of wood
or the organ left unclaimed
by one missing link or another
that will adjust to the soul
when the era
of another adventurous life begins
I comply
and I search
I synchronise my disorder to the world's disorder
I write so as not to lose myself, so as not to fall
I write while looking feverishly at my watch
the trajectory of the sun
the shadow cast on the wall
I search through the polluted sand
right to the tip of the round wood
the slightest burst of white stone

I spy the birds that perch
so I can go argue with them over that famous seed
I dig into my arteries
to find some organ
which school never taught me existed
By the way, answer me this
how can one find a black stone in the dark?

I write, regardless of whether I have nothing or everything
the vitality of despair
and God knows this is so vast
I work as hard as a poor stonemason
whom fate has tasked with building the palaces of the rich
as hard as a miner who digs into the belly of the earth
to avenge his sterility
which he doubtlessly reproaches his wife for

I write like other people pray
or atone for their sins
and I accept the Mystery
Sometimes I even experience the same joys they do
the same marvels
but I often think they ignore
the torments that give my prayers
the touches of truth that defy faith

I write
when you write to me
O word
and I add details that elude you
when I submit your words to the ordeal
awaken in them the memory that predates you
When I stop treating them like slaves
and I caress them with a sense of dignity

When I fix a date for our amorous rendezvous
and show up early to savour the ecstasy of expectation
When I invite them after the obligatory drink
to a meal where we eat with our fingers
from the same plate
When I demand nothing of them
except our duty
to our sovereign freedom
I write out of compassion
holding out my beggar's bowl
and who cares if all I collect is a bunch of spit

O Word
look at how you've hardened me
I've become your anvil
The hammers of the world can strike down
but I will not shirk
I'll wait until they tire themselves out
to prepare myself for the world to come
Which will have its own hammers, no doubt!

Did I get any sleep my love
What did I say about the things I thought I saw
Where did this hair
I tied around my tongue come from
Why am I all stiff?
My feet are swollen
My head feels like all the heavy water spilled out
But now I'm suddenly peaceful
ready to see and listen
to slip out of your embrace
and to appear before the Scales
to weigh my soul
and whatever the palms of my hands have owned

and deposit the few feathers left on my wings
the embroidered handkerchief I forgot in my pocket
My body will be naked except for our wedding band
Neither angels nor demons will take that away from me
I will fight tooth and nail to keep it
with the rage of an invalid
I will defend it
and like in the old stories
I will spin it around my finger
when the jailer thinks he's cut off all exits
There will be thunder and great tower of smoke
a tremor, and a partridge will make an unexpected flight
And the miracle will be there
our heartbeats will pulse along peacefully
and play their symphony
wrist against wrist
while we float
atop the span of our island
with a new inventory of words
a little drinking water
some fruit
knowing that our little skiff belongs to this world
which is crumbling around us
within us
Our skiff is of this world
which is even more lost than we are
Our skiff is of this world
dumbfounded
because it's either too young or too old
to understand
that a little ring
can perform a miracle

Dreams Come to Die on the Page

One by one
dreams come to die on the page
The news made the rounds
and they came from all corners
to die on the page
like elephants travelling to their graveyards
I witnessed their death-throes
unable to hold out a glass of water
I looked at them for the first time
and for the last time
before wrapping them in the funerary shroud of my speech
and stretching them out on the little boat
that once was their cradle
The current sweeps them away
and quickly brings them back to me
as if the wide-open sea wasn't out there
but right here on the page

There's a Cannibal Who Reads Me

There's a cannibal who reads me
A ferociously intelligent reader
a reader of dreams
not a word slips past him
without his considering its weight in blood
He even does away with all the commas
in order to find the choicest bits
He knows that the page resonates
with the splendid tremor of breath
Oh that turmoil that makes the prey
so mouthwatering and ready to submit
He waits for fatigue
to slip over my face
like a sacrificial mask
He searches for the faults and rifts to slip in
a superfluous adjective
an unforgivable repetition
There's a cannibal who reads me
so he can feed himself

I'm a Child of this Century

I'm a child of this dreary century
a child who never grew up
Doubts that set my tongue on fire
burned my wings
I learned to walk
then I unlearned it
I grew weary of oases
and camels eager for ruins
My head turned to the East
I lie in the middle of the road
and wait for the caravan of the mad

My Mother's Language

It's been twenty years since I last saw my mother
She starved herself to death
They say that each morning
she would pull her headscarf off
and strike the floor seven times
cursing the heavens and the Tyrant
I was in the cave
where convicts read in the dark
and painted the bestiary of the future on the walls
It's been twenty years since I last saw my mother
She left me a china coffee set
and though the cups have broken one by one
they were so ugly I didn't regret their loss
even though coffee's the only drink I like
These days, when I'm alone
I start to sound like my mother
or rather, it's as if she were using my mouth
to voice her profanities, curses and gibberish
the unfindable rosary of her nicknames
all the endangered species of her sayings
It's been twenty years since I last saw my mother
but I am the last man
who still speaks her language

One Hand Isn't Enough to Write

One hand isn't enough to write
These days
it takes two
and the second quickly needs to grasp
the craft of the unspeakable:
to embroider the name of a star
that will rise after the next apocalypse
to see the unbreakable thread among thousands
to weave from the fabric of passions
swaddling bands, overcoats, winding cloths
to carve a beginning from a pile of waste
Two hands aren't enough to write
These days
with its grinding miseries
it would take three or four
for life to bother visiting
this white wretched wasteland

The Wolves

I hear the wolves
nice and snug in their country homes
staring gluttonously at their televisions
counting bodies out loud
howling at the top of their lungs
for hours on end
I see the wolves
without their sheep's clothing
stuff their faces with fresh game
elect their token Judas by show of hands
drink the blood of a village
that is still young, a little fruity
the blood of a land strewn with mass graves
for hours on end
I hear the wolves
turn the lights off at midnight
and lawfully rape their wives

In Vain I Migrate

I migrate in vain
In every city I drink the same coffee
and resign myself to the waiter's impassive face
The laughter of nearby tables
disturbs the evening's music
A woman walks by for the last time
In vain I migrate
ensuring my own alienation
I find the same crescent moon in every sky
and the stubborn silence of the stars
In my sleep I speak
a medley of languages
and animal calls
The room where I wake
is the one I was born in
I migrate in vain
The secret of birds eludes me
as does my suitcase's magnet
which springs open
at each stage of the journey

Two Hours on a Train

On a two-hour train ride
I replay the film of my life
Roughly two minutes per year
A half hour for my childhood
another for my time in prison
While love, books and travels
share the rest
My partner's hand gradually
fuses into my own and her head,
which rests on my shoulder
feels as light as a dove
By the time we'll arrive
I'll have reached my fifties
and I'll have little over an hour
left to live

The Manuscript

I had no idea that Satan (or Iblis to his friends) was a midget, a gossip and a thief to boot.

I was writing at my desk when he came and sat beside me. I'm no giant, but I was a full head taller than him. I was easily able look him over and make out his distinctive features one by one. In profile, his nose appeared to be long. His one eye had no lashes. A seven-pointed star was tattooed at the corner of his lips.

Having thus examined and recognised him, I returned calmly to work. Well, well, a poem about Iblis, I said to myself. The minute I had this thought my companion reacted. I watched a very slender hand emerge from his pocket and place itself on my sheet of paper. Whenever I wrote a word, he immediately added another – with what I must say was a real sense of appropriateness. But if I didn't like one of his ideas and deleted it, he immediately responded in kind to one of mine.

We wrote and edited for a long time until the phone began to ring. I picked it up and waited for someone to speak. But there was no one there. I slammed the phone down.

Iblis had taken advantage of this interlude to vanish, taking our manuscript along with him.

I've Just Returned from the Sea

I've just returned from the sea where a mermaid had dragged me off so she could make love to me in a way that would make the Gods blush. Her magic didn't work on me because I've got my own obsessions, just like everyone else. I need a room with the door shut, or at least a car with the doors locked. The slightest noise spoils the whole pleasure.

Still, down there, in that underwater metropolis which I immediately proclaimed was the lost capital of Atlantis, the houses had no doors and nobody used curtains. Outside, an awful war pitted the Bearded Ones, who longed for freshwater, and the Clean-Shaven Ones, who were obsessed with saltwater. The terrible clash of weapons muffled my mermaid's little cries, who sadly for her, had feet made of ice.

So I plugged my ears and plunged into my oily dream, just like my ancestor, Ulysses.

Burn the Midnight Oil

You must stay up all night at least four times a year.

There aren't enough crazy people around me to go further than that. A single sleepless night isn't worth much when you're on your own. It needs to be shared. Only then does the city open up to you without thoughts of death. Gargoyles carry out their work as exorcists. Muezzins get drunk on street corners. There is always a couple who get married at dawn by drawing lots. The Partisans' Chant* becomes a drinking song. Satan starts to wax lyrical and hands out unbaited red apples to the worshippers. Feet trample on a treasure-hoard of stars. The taste of sex rises in the mouth like lemon on oysters.

Only vagabonds can be poets.

---

* 'The Partisans' Chant' or 'Chant des Partisans' was the most popular song of the French Resistance during World War II. –Tr.

The Elegant Sufi

When the Sufi discovered English wool, cashmere, and silk scarves, he tore off his coarse woollen robe and said to himself: 'I'll feel more comfortable wearing these cloths. They will make my genuflections more graceful. I'm going to cut my hair and trim my beard, brush my teeth three times a day, use a good Eau de Cologne as a deodorant, chuck my tattered prayer mat away and replace it with a genuine Zemmour rug.* I will show myself neat and tidy in front of God and I dare say my prayers will become purer. Henceforth, I will no longer live on alms. I'm going to find myself honest and honourable work. I will mingle among my kind, become acquainted with their preoccupations, find out about their blasphemies and initiate myself into the secrets of their terrestrial attachments, taste their earthly wines, and little by little lead them back to the path of the Mystery. After all, my life would only have changed in an outward way, but I will have paved a new path towards mysticism, that of the elegant Sufis.'

* Zemmour: name of a Berber tribe in the Middle Atlas whose handmade carpets are highly sought after. – Tr.

The Word-Gulag

They've opened a new gulag. The word-gulag.

I go there every week, and take a shopping bag filled with fresh fruit, a bar of soap and a few tins of condensed milk. I call out a prisoner's name at random, then wait in the visitors' room with the gesturing crowd. One by one, the words file out of a little door and stand in front of us on the other side of the wire. Pale. Trembling. Haggard. Shattered.

'Speak!' the guard barks while he patrols the corridor that divides us, clanging his keys against the grill.

No one responds. The words can't reply because their jaws are visibly broken. Nor can the visitors because, as they've just suddenly realised – they really should have wised up to this earlier – the gulag has robbed them of all their best words.

'Visiting time is over', the guard shouts, drawing a curtain we hadn't noticed before.

Some barely audible words burst out, but nobody could tell which side of the grill they were coming from. They were probably words of goodbye.

The Poem-Tree

I am the poem-tree. Scientists say I belong to an endangered species, but nobody seems to care, despite the recent appeals launched to save the Red Panda and the African Elephant.

Some say it's a question of public interest, but I say it's a question of memory. From time to time, the memory of men reaches saturation point, when they offload the heavy weight of the past and make room to prepare for the beloved new.

These days, old species aren't fashionable. They have invented trees that grow quickly and make do with only water and sunshine, and who go about being trees both quietly and soullessly.

I am the poem-tree. They have tried to manipulate me, but their efforts came to naught; I'm intractable, the master of my own mutations. Seasonal and epochal changes don't bother me. The fruits I bear are never the same. Sometimes I fill them with nectar, and other times with bile; and when I spy a predator from afar, I riddle him with thorns.

Occasionally I ask myself: am I really a tree? Then I become afraid of walking, of speaking the sad language of this dishonest species. I grab hold of an axe and cut down my weakest neighbour's trunk. So I cling to my roots with all my strength. Inside their endless veins, I follow the stream of words right up to the primordial cry and break through the labyrinth of languages. I grasp the skein end and pull on it to free light and music. An image reveals itself to me. I produce buds that please me and look forward to the flowers. All this occurs under cover of night, with the help of the stars and rare birds that have chosen freedom.

I am the poem-tree. I chuckle at all things ephemeral and eternal.

I am alive.

Life

Life
It's enough I woke up
the sun to my right
the moon to my left
and that I walked
from my mother's womb
to the threshold of this century
Life
It's enough I tasted this fruit
I wrote about what I witnessed
I never kept quiet about the horrors
I did all I could
and everything I took, I gave over to love
Life
is nothing short of a miracle
that nobody sees
O wounded body
wounded soul
Admit you've been happy
Just between us
admit it

FROM

Write Life

(2005)

Far from Baghdad

Crash of boots
Ishmael
is back in the place of the ram
God has changed his mind
and Abraham's tears
fall in vain.
The butchers are here.

We are lost
shocked
like dromedaries
in the desert of Iraq
who watch a caravan
of armoured cars pass by

That water
is bought and sold
is understood
It's just that now
it's also used
to launder consciences

After the grave robbers
here come the museum-looters
Behold progress!

The statue was beheaded
It was only a lump
of bronze or steel
But in the heads of man

nothing has changed
The tyrant is dead
Long live the tyrant!

Freedom's torn apart
Have we repeated everything
like parrots?
The same old refrain is over
Know this
freedom imposes itself

'If I don't kill you, I'm doing you a favour', goes an old Moroccan saying. Some pearls of wisdom send shivers down your spine.

'Only lend to the rich', the French saying goes. In Arabic slang this turns into 'Fatten the ass of a fat sheep'! Happy now, translator?

We only talk about banning weapons of mass destruction. And what about weapons of partial destruction?

Given the amount of human blood spilled every day, I'm astonished that none of these multinationals have tried to turn it into a new source of energy.

Mass graves unearthed
filmed
from every angle
Strange booty

Near a charred vehicle
corpses are trampled
smiles on their lips

Even in hatred
there's something grotesque

Are some assassins more noble than others?

So many poets stopped here
before other ruins
after other ravages
But they at least
had only one idea in their heads
to improvise new love songs

For every woman
who adopts
or readopts the veil
that's ten years
of progress
gone up in smoke

Basra
Thirty years ago
The most potent arak
flowed freely
The poets gathered
to laugh beneath the stars
awash with their visions
That traitorous arak!

Somewhere round here
Wisdom
had its house
Aristotle was rescued from oblivion
Scheherazade conceived
the mother of all stories

The spirit breathed
until it ran out of breath
before succumbing
to suffocating pollution
caused by the 'mother of all wars'

A people can only outwit their oppressor if they're morally superior

A cradle of humanity
shall we say
It's hardly surprising
here or elsewhere
that predators are recruited
from this very cradle

But you could say
that the oppressed
are eager to usurp
the oppressor
to punish in turn
those who came first
or else themselves

Despite his wisdom, the great Ibn Khaldun failed to grasp this
fundamental twist of universal history

When the moral is uncorked
we must drink down to the dregs

See the unspeakable and die

In the belly of the night
a cry rises
but where does it go?

The seven heavens
sucked into a black hole
have rejoined the queue
of the helpless

The Earth Opens and Welcomes You

i.m. Tahar Djaout *

The earth opens
and welcomes you
Why these cries, these tears
these prayers
What have they lost
What are they looking for
those who disturb
your new-found peace?

The earth opens
and welcomes you
Now
you're going to speak without witnesses
O, you've got plenty to say
and you'll have all eternity
The words tarnished by yesterday's tumults
will gradually burn in silence

The earth opens
and welcomes you
She alone desired you
without you making a move
She waited with none of Penelope's guile
Her patience was nothing but kindness
and it's kindness that brought you back to her

The earth opens
and welcomes you
She will not ask you to render accounts

of your fleeting affairs
wandering girls
heavenly bodies of flesh conceived in the eyes
fruits gifted by the vast orchards of life
sovereign passions that shine
in your palm's hollow
at the end of an indifferent language

The earth opens
and welcomes you
You're naked
And she's more naked than you
You're both beautiful
in that silent embrace
where hands can restrain themselves
and steer clear of violence
where the butterfly of the soul
avoids this semblance of light
to go in search of its origins

The earth opens
and welcomes you
One day, your beloved will rediscover
your legendary smile
and the mourning will end
Your children will grow up
and boldly read your poems
Your country will heal, almost magically
when men consumed by the illusion
will drink from the fountain of your kindness

O my friend
sleep well

you deserve it
because you worked hard
like an honourable man

Before you left
you cleaned up your office
left everything neatly arranged
You switched off the lights
and on stepping out
looked up at the sky
which was almost too painfully blue
You smoothed your moustache
and said to yourself:
only cowards
think that death is the end

Sleep well my friend
Sleep the sleep of the righteous
Rest well
from your dreams too
Let us shoulder the burden a little

★ Tahar Djaout (1954-1993): Algerian writer murdered by Islamic
  extremists in Algiers in 1993, at the height of the civil war. The
  poem was written on the day of his burial. – Tr.

Dish of the Day

For today's special
we'd like to recommend a very spicy
'killer' stew
The innkeeper
didn't look like he was joking
You won't need a starter, he added
as the stew is very substantial
a local wine
the kind used for sangria
We'll mash a freshly-
plucked eyeball
'Cain's', the innkeeper
said to be precise
believing he'd excelled himself
with his use black humour
O you know, I said,
I'm just a little peckish
would you mind if
I looked at the menu again please?

False Expectations

What actually happens
always defies our expectations
Which is as unchanging a law
as that of gravity
Unless one of these days
science shows us
that the opposite is true
Which would surprise me

Fingerprints

If only we could write
simply by pressing
our fingerprints
on the page
this would avoid
the harm we cause ourselves
in our quest to be original

FROM

Another Morocco

(2013)

The Day Hassan II Died

Hassan II ruled Morocco from 1961 until his death in 1999. His era – now referred to as the 'years of lead' – was characterized by jingoism and social repression, which included the incarceration and murder of thousands of dissidents. The ascension of Hassan II's eldest son Mohammed VI to the throne in 1999 marked the beginning of momentous social changes in the country, with steps being taken to rein in the monarchy's powers and establish some basic rights. – Tr.

*

Then the day arrived: 23 July 1999, that surreal day when I learned of the death of Hassan II. I was travelling in the South of France, and my oldest son Yacine called to tell me the news. When I think of how he described his own reaction, it still causes me to shudder. 'You know, Dad,' he said, 'that day when they came and took you from our home to interrogate you and then throw you in jail, it felt like an iron bar entered my body and lodged itself between my shoulders. All this time, I've lived without daring to open up to you, as if that bar were preventing me from breathing. And today, suddenly, it has slid right back out of me. At last, it feels as if I can breathe again!'

That is how an adult, who was only seven years old when his father was taken from him, reacted to the announcement of Hassan II's death. His account seems infinitely more powerful than anything that I could manage to say about my state of mind in that moment.

But let us not dwell on the past! May the dead rest in peace, even if some among them turned the lives of their fellow men into a bottomless hell.

Mohammed VI's reign began on the eve of a new century which ushered in a new millennium. It was a fitting coincidence. Why didn't we realise the clear sign that History was sending us, prompting us to contemplate previous rendezvous that we had missed time and time again? The most significant one of late was misleadingly called 'reformist government'.[1] When Hassan II, weakened by a long illness, loosened his firm grip on the country's politics, certain individuals, including men of integrity like Abderrahmane Youssoufi, stood for election at their own risk. They took on that responsibility in the belief perhaps that their political engagement would lay the groundwork for a true laboratory of democracy. What they seemed to have forgotten, despite their long experience and full knowledge of the Makhzen's[2] capabilities, was its unchanging mentality, its truly self-serving machinations, and its unmatched ability to manipulate. The transition that those men of integrity tried to bring to fruition quickly foundered, as it lacked an appropriate strategy or the resolution to implement it.

Such shortcomings might have been understandable while they were dealing with their old, intransigent adversary, but what is less understandable is why they went ahead once the obstacle was removed and the transition period provided distinct and unparallelled room for action. At that point, it became possible to establish a new balance of power and new rules to the game. There even existed a genuine possibility for a formal agreement on democratic transition along with the constitutional changes necessary to put it in place.

I remain convinced that such a story truly had a chance of being written at the beginning of Mohammed VI's reign. The political game had opened up considerably, and it seemed likely that its rules would be decided collectively and no longer, as they were in the past, by a single man.

In this respect, I can't help but think of the exemplary success of the Spanish democratic transition in the wake of Franco's death. It is true that the success there was, on the one hand, the labour of established opposition movements steeped in the relentless struggle against the dictatorship, and, on the other hand, that of exceptional men of state such as King Juan Carlos and Prime Minister Adolfo Suarez. As has often been said before, these fortuitous rendezvous with History are often facilitated by key figures of exceptional political instinct. Such men are motivated by a vision that is both forward-looking and yet still in harmony with the reality of the moment in which great changes are required. Without meaning to offend, I do believe that such dispositions have been painfully lacking in our country, an absence that, sadly, continues even to this day.

Instead of insisting on a transition negotiated in the greatest possible transparency with the aim of establishing the rule of law and reforming the monarchy itself, the reformist government contented itself with studies of issues and preparation of reforms whose execution was supposedly within its jurisdiction but for which it rarely dared to assume full responsibility. When the tables turned, it still continued to interact with the Makhzen as it had under the preceding regime. The most instructive example of its lack of cunning, initiative, and political resolution is given to us by its handling of one of the period's major issues: the reform of the Mudawana.[3] Brought to the public's attention thanks to feminists' long struggle and then single-handedly drafted as a law by one courageous minister, the reform encountered the law of equivocation which marked that government's action. The end result was that the man of conviction was disowned and the reform was taken from him by the Chief of State who, in promulgating the law, passed as its initiator, thus reaping all its moral and symbolic benefit.

In any event, disillusioned hopes are commonplace in our history. Transitions that take us nowhere. Supposedly 'democratic' processes which do nothing but stall, like broken-down engines that never should have left the factory floor. At the beginning of the new millennium, we were still at the cross-roads, not knowing which path to take, or rather, not knowing which path our government had already taken unbeknownst to us. We were entitled to governance where the new and the old cacophonously coexisted, where rumour served as information, and where fortune-tellers were more sought after than experienced political organisers. Having not been consulted about the future they were crafting for us, we grasped at the slightest sign that might have provided a clue about their plans.

That's why the symbolic, but non-negligible, measures that marked the young king's reign seemed such good omens. There were several well-known measures that I was quick to note as they happened: the attention given to the population in the north of the country – especially in the Rif – with the goal of redressing the injustices suffered during Hassan II's reign, the introduction of human rights cases in the Equality and Reconciliation Court, the Mudawana reform in the circumstances I described above, the decisions taken in favour of Amazigh language and culture, the authorisation of Abraham Serfaty's return from exile,[4] and the dismissal of Driss Basri, the infamous Minister of the Interior.[5] Beyond those measures, we might add other 'details' that eluded many observers or somehow didn't seem important enough to note and assess their full importance. There is no lack of examples, like the decision to close the royal harem and send its members back to their families or the order to the media to cease broadcasting supposedly patriotic songs glorifying the deceased king, thus discouraging flattering artists from reoffending by venerating his successor.

I may be mistaken, but I believe that the questions on everyone's minds were the following: Deep down had the monarch recognised the sufferings we had endured during his predecessor's reign? Had he decided to redress those injustices in transparency and justice? Would his sensitivity, peculiar to youth, push him to establish a break with the methods of the past? Would it then hopefully lead him to reject inherited institutional archaisms and to opt for a monarchical model more consistent with this modern era's demands? Consequently, would he contemplate changing his own status to become a loyal partner to the nation's dynamic forces implementing democracy?

In the midst of our self-questioning, I published a text entitled 'Don't Squander the Hope' in an effort to share my thoughts on the 'possibility of the impossible' that I hoped to see come to pass. In that text I affirmed, in short, that our country was still at the crossroads and that a new page had opened in its history. The crucial question subsequently raised was: What story would we write? Two paths were possible. The first, a continuation of the path of the former regime, led assuredly to a dead-end, since its supporters had not given up their arms and they retained the ability to impede progress. The second was nothing other than pure imagination, a total renewal of mind and of political practices. It required courage and the mobilisation of the country's men and women. Because only a break with the methods of the past would enable the country to exit out of the economic, social, and moral horror afflicting it. At that exact moment, I conjectured that the king himself had encountered this fork in the road and that he had come out in favour of the second path. For that choice, though, some prerequisites were necessary. In my opinion, the transition towards democracy would require a re-foundation of the Constitution. The new one would no longer be handed down to us like the preceding ones, rubber-stamped by a referendum whose result was known in advance. No, only a sovereign constitutional assembly, elected by universal, legitimate, and transparent suffrage, could take on this task whose primordial concern was to establish the separation of powers with a re-balancing benefiting the executive and the legislative branches.

In advancing that idea, I was aware that the ballot box ran the risk of turning its back on democracy, but I believed all would depend on the work to be accomplished in the interim: a task that was incumbent, above all, on democrats and which would not be accomplished without rallying grassroots movements, which, for decades, had fought for the establishment of rule of law and against oppression and the arbitrary exercise of force. Furthermore, I called for local councils of all the democratic forces in Morocco: an Estates General that would have allowed for the development of a Democratic Pact specifying the requirements for a true transition to democracy.

The page that opened at that moment in our history was not written as I would have liked. At the crossroads, we did nothing more than shuffle. And, as we well know, a failure to go forward is, in itself, a step backwards.

Translated by Christopher Schaefer

1 In 1998, after decades in opposition and in exile, the Socialist Abderrahmane Youssofi was named as Prime Minister in a power-sharing agreement that kept the king's right-hand man Driss Basri as Minister of the Interior.

2 An Arabic word meaning 'warehouse' or 'shop', used in Morocco to signify the elite civil servants that directly represent the king and his power.

3 The *Mudawana* is the family code in Moroccan law, which was reformed in 2004. It regulates issues related to marriage such as minimum legal age, divorce, and polygamy. The only section of Moroccan law that relies primarily on Islamic sources rather than Spanish or French civil codes, it was meant to unify the country under a modern Islamic identity.

4 Abraham Serfaty was an anti-Zionist Moroccan Jew and prominent dissident who collaborated with Laâbi on *Souffles* and was imprisoned for seventeen years for his political activities. After being released from prison he went into exile in France.

5 In Morocco, the Ministry of the Interior is perhaps the most powerful as it controls the country's internal security.

Interview

An Interview with Abdellatif Laâbi

In May 2013, Christopher Schaefer sat down with Abdellatif Laâbi at his home in Créteil, on the outskirts of Paris, to discuss, among other topics, his literary career, his profound love for his decidedly un-literary parents, Morocco's complicated linguistic and political situation, and Moroccan rap.

*

CS: *The Bottom of the Jar*, which has just been published in English translation, describes your childhood, and in various other books and articles you have written about your imprisonment in Morocco and then exile in France. Can you speak a little about what occurred between those two events, the beginning of your literary career, your introduction to fellow poet Mohamed Khaïr-Eddine, and the decision to launch the literary journal *Souffles*?

AL: Yes, that was in 1965. I had started writing and publishing in several literary magazines here in France, and also in Moroccan reviews. And then I discovered that there was a group of young poets in Casablanca publishing some small reviews called *Poésie toute* and *Eaux vives*. And they also published in the automobile magazine of Casablanca. That gives you an idea of the limited options at the time when it came to literary reviews. So we met – or rather, I was curious enough to seek them out – and at the same time we met a group of painters in Casablanca: Mohamed Melehi, Mohamed Chebaa, and Farid Belkahia. Farid was the Director of the Ecoles de Beaux Arts in Casablanca, and the two others taught there. So that was the group we started with: Mostafa Nissaboury (the other poet), Mohamed Khaïr-Eddine, and then the painters from Casablanca. I think it's very important to note that *Souffles* began with a group of poets and artists/painters, which is something that gave it a completely original character, perhaps unique in the history of Moroccan literary reviews up to that time. There weren't just new texts compared with the literature of the time, but also a plastic and graphic conception that was unprecedented. The painters had studied in countries such as Czechoslovakia, the United States, Italy, and Spain. So they all arrived with a diverse set of perspectives and skill sets, and, furthermore, they were on that same quest for modernity that we poets were on. So that's the context in which *Souffles* was founded. I didn't see Mohamed Khaïr-Eddine but three or four times perhaps, because he left very quickly for France, where he began to publish his books. It was Mostafa Nissaboury more than anyone else who accompanied the review the longest – almost to its very end.

CS: Mohamed Khaïr-Eddine was in Agadir just after the 1960 earthquake, if I'm not mistaken.

AL: Yes. After working in Agadir in the aftermath of the earthquake he left for Casablanca, where he wrote *Agadir*, his first novel.

CS: *The Bottom of the Jar* begins and ends with a small anecdote about your father's response to televised reports of the fall of the Berlin Wall. At the very end, your father humorously compares Berlin to Fez, saying 'Bahh, is that the only news they could find to tell us! A falling wall… it can't have been built very solidly. The walls of Fez are still standing after all.' In your writings about your parents, they possess a certain kind of, we might say, uneducated wisdom. Do you agree that type of wisdom is being lost? And, if so, what does it consist of?

AL: In *The Bottom of the Jar* I recount several years of my childhood, from the age of seven or eight until the struggle for Moroccan independence in 1952 and 1953. At the same time, it's an homage to my father and my mother. My father and my mother didn't know how to read or write. But that didn't mean that they didn't have a culture or that the popular language that they spoke was a language reduced to the level of its expressive capabilities. I have from time to time reflected on how I ended up writing. What pushed me to write? What was the trigger? More and more, the image of my mother imposes itself on me, because she was a woman who had a rich language, full of images, and a great sense of humour. She was often angry at her condition, and it was by listening to her speak that perhaps – and I say perhaps – the desire to write was born in me. So, there is this homage, of course, to that woman who had eleven children, three of whom died – so eight children: three brothers and four sisters who survived. The ten of us lived in a small house of two rooms. My father was a simple craftsman who worked his entire life. My mother worked for us her entire life. It seemed they were almost slaves in our service, so that we could eat, so that we could be clothed, and so that we could go to school. All of that touches me very deeply – to see a man and a woman at that moment in time, in their condition, illiterate – who spent their entire life for us. And that's why they appear not just in *The Bottom of the Jar*, but also in other books of mine.

CS: Something that struck me while reading your autobiography was that your first encounter with the French language was via an Algerian teacher of French, Mr Benaïssa. Do you know what happened to him afterward? Did he return to Algeria? Did he fight in the Algerian War of Independence? Did he emigrate to France?

AL: No, not at all. In fact, during the colonial period, there were a great many Algerians who came to Morocco because they were translators for the French colonial administration or they taught. Already in Algeria there was a Frenchified elite because the colonisation there dated from 1830, whereas in Morocco it was much more recent.

CS: Do you read English a little?

AL: I spoke English well until my high school graduation. Afterwards, unfortunately, I didn't use it regularly.

CS: Have you read André Naffis-Sahely's translation?

AL: Yes, I looked at it a little.

CS: Did you work together at all?

AL: No. He worked freely. Occasionally he asked me for small clarifications, but the translation was his own work, which, according to many of my Anglophone friends, is excellent.

CS: Which Moroccan writers deserve a wider readership in the English-speaking world? That is, which Moroccan writers who have not yet been translated into English deserve translation?

AL: Unfortunately, I find that notably in the United States, but also in Great Britain, there is not a great deal of interest in Arabic literature, Moroccan literature included, whether in Arabic or French, with only few exceptions, Tahar Ben Jelloun for example, or Driss Chraïbi.

CS: Paul Bowles translated Mohammed Choukri...

AL: Yes, Mohammed Choukri. But... I find that in other countries, for example, in Spain or even in Germany, there is a much greater interest. In the United States translation of national literatures remains rather limited in comparison to what is translated in France or in other countries like the Netherlands or even in Turkey. And it's true that in the English-speaking world, translation is a lot less important than in the old Europe [laughter]. There are many Moroccan writers who deserve translation. We have some great poets, for example. Unfortunately, when it comes to poetry, it's even more complicated, even rarer to see books of poetry translated in the United States. There would be a couple dozen authors...

CS: A couple dozen... could you give some examples?

AL: There is Driss Chraïbi, who hasn't been translated very much, at least not enough. There are also French-language writers like Mahi Binebine, Fouad Laroui, Mohammed Leftah, etc. Poets like Mostafa Nissaboury. Writers in Arabic like Mohamed Zefzaf, Driss Khoury, Mohamed Berrada, Mohamed Achaari, Mohamed Bennis, and Abdelkrim Tabbal, one of our great poets, and that's all without speaking of Amazigh [Berber] writers or those who write in our dialect of Arabic. I compiled an anthology of Moroccan poetry about ten years ago that comprised texts by fifty Moroccan poets.

CS: Since independence, right?

AL: Yes, since independence. Poets who write either in French or in Classical Arabic or in Arabic dialect or in Amazigh. That book could give an idea, at least when it comes to poetry.

CS: Another question that is often posed to you is that of your decision to write in French. Your typical response is that it is a complicated issue. You mention Salman Rushdie, whose mother tongue is Urdu but who writes in English...

AL: Samuel Beckett, the Irish man who also wrote in French...

CS: Yes, exactly.

AL: Personally I believe the question has become a little absurd. Today there is a globalisation of literature. And furthermore, we can pose the same question to any good reader of literature. In his or her reading, eighty percent of the books are probably translations. You haven't read Tolstoy or Dostoevsky in Russian, at least so far as I know [laughter], or Kawabata or

Murakami in Japanese. It's like that. It's a question that doesn't really mean very much in my opinion. The language in which a writer writes is one which he chooses voluntarily. Either it's his mother tongue or it's the language that was imposed on him at some point because history wanted it. In North Africa, because of the French colonial presence, there were three generations of Algerian, Tunisian, and Moroccan writers who wrote in French. What is important is not the language in which they write but what they do with that language, how they work with the French language. Does their mother tongue disappear the moment they write? It's a good question and it must be raised. What must be done with these writers is to see how the different linguistic registers are moulded into their writing. That's perhaps what makes the particular soul, the breath, and the musicality of those writings. It's because they are moulded by two or three languages at the same time, even if they are enunciated at the end of the day in French.

CS: I completely agree with you. For me though, my mother tongue is the same language used in media and in education. There isn't a great deal of variation between the dialect and the elevated educated form. And that's why it's often difficult for Americans or others from similar situations to understand the diversity and complexity of the linguistic situation in Morocco.

AL: One of the concerns of *The Bottom of the Jar* is a linguistic concern. In that book I tried to perfectly map the French language onto the Arabic language, without it becoming a bastard tongue.

CS: I began my studies as a medievalist, and one of the key moments in medieval literature is an essay by Dante entitled *Du vulgari eloquentia* (*On the Eloquence of the Common Tongue*) in which he advocates the use of Italian in place of Latin, which was used at that time for religion, education, etc. And something I wondered when I was in Morocco was whether there will be a moment like that for Darija (the Moroccan dialect of Arabic). Will the time come when someone says, 'we must write poetry in Moroccan Arabic because it can be just as eloquent'? I know that there are poets and writers that have already begun this work, but do you find that Moroccan Arabic has already undergone the pivotal moment that Italian experienced with Dante or are we still waiting for it?

AL: I believe we are still a long way off. I've thought a great deal about the linguistic situation in Morocco and I have tried to kindle a debate around this question. What is the issue? It's to know in what languages we're going to be writing in twenty or thirty years. In what languages – and I say 'languages' in the plural – are we going to teach? That is the fundamental concern. And yet there is an ideological discourse surrounding the languages: the attachment of the Arabisers to Arabic is an ideological attachment, and it's the same thing for the Amazighs and those who defend Darija. I say simply: instead of beating each other up over this or that language, we must begin to bring all these national languages up to speed. We must prepare them so that they truly become languages of creation, of teaching, of scientific research, and of communication at the same time. And yet this work has not been done since Moroccan independence. We don't cease to change directions, either Arabising or French-ifying, and we have lost a great deal of time – instead of telling ourselves, Okay, we have to prepare these languages, first the three national languages I already mentioned [Darija, Classical Arabic and Amazigh]. We must prepare them so that they can become languages where we express ourselves, we have the same means as someone who uses Spanish, Italian, and English. That right there is the real issue. I personally believe that we have to prepare the ground. There isn't for example a true dictionary for Darija. There is a grammar that was done during the colonial era by the French, but it isn't used anymore. And yet a part of the language is in the process of disappearing, because there is a new Darija. You know, because you lived in Morocco.

You see how we absurdly mix French and Arabic. Same thing for Amazigh, which is inscribed in the constitution as a national language, but which suffers from the same problems as Darija. Same thing for Classical Arabic, which does not even have an etymological dictionary, for example. It's a huge lacuna. How can we work with words whose origin and evolution we don't know? It's a real handicap.

CS: I think this is a good moment to speak a little about your recent book *Un autre Maroc* (*Another Morocco*) and your political engagement. When I was in Morocco, an article of yours was published in the magazine *TelQuel* where you put forth certain theses for Morocco. Now you seem to be taking a more hands-on approach, publishing full-length books and launching an organisation...

AL: No, I'm not a politician. I'm a writer and an intellectual, but an intellectual who defends his right to have his own analysis of the political situation of his country or of the world and also to have ideas, propositions, and a vision for the future. We have often marginalised intellectuals as if they weren't full citizens. I personally assert the right of intellectuals to have opinions about politics and to defend them, without being inserted in a political party or in some sort of organisation. The political class in Morocco, as in many other countries, even in advanced democracies, has lost a great deal of credibility. And yet the intellectual has an opportunity to keep his freedom of speech, to say truthfully what he thinks. Even if it's against the consensus. The intellectual is not required to be in the consensus. That's something extremely valuable in my opinion, that every kind of country contains men and women with that freedom of thought.

CS: I understand that well. But you have also just stated that Darija and Amazigh need to be developed. And for that it requires an educational system in place. And if changes are needed in the educational system, you don't need a political project necessarily, but political measures.

AL: Yes, a political project is required, of course. I'm saying that I can venture ideas, and in my last book *Un autre Maroc*, I do just that: I make propositions. Because I consider that we have spoken too long of democracy – the vocabulary and the lexicon. You, who have lived in Morocco for a long time, have no doubt remarked that the political class, the mixture of tendencies – right and left – has mastered the lexicon of democracy, of transparency, of good governance, of human rights, etc., but there is a true gap between discourse and reality. Personally, I think that in Morocco we are not yet in democracy. There is the idea of a democratic project, but, for me, the cornerstone of that democratic project is a genuine revolution in our educational system. In Morocco we live in a kind of apartheid when it comes to education and teaching. Public education is for the people and private education is reserved for those who have the means to pay and then later send their kids abroad for college. We suffer from a genuine apartheid there. Eighty percent of young Moroccans receive public education. It's a third-rate education that has been emptied completely of its content. It doesn't form free citizens, youths capable of thinking for themselves. It doesn't prepare them to think critically, and surely not to hold a job someday. It prepares the majority of children who go to school for unemployment. So in my opinion we cannot speak of democracy until the moment when we have put an end to this system of apartheid. At that moment, yes, we will have genuine citizens. School is where we form citizens, where we form democrats, individuals attached to democracy, to human rights, to humanist values that guard them against intolerance and extremism. That's what I propose. But for me today, the political class as it exists is no longer capable of leading the fight for genuine democracy. In *Un autre Maroc* I call for the formation of a new citizen force capable of leading this fight. We have a 100-year-old political class. We need the youth of today to take on that responsibility. We need women to take on political responsibilities. We need civil society to be engaged in that combat. We need intellectuals, thinkers, and researchers who can also be engaged in this fight.

CS: Have you been in contact with the leaders of the February 20th Movement? [The protest movement in Morocco during the Arab Spring.]

AL: Yes, of course.

CS: Have they sought you out?

AL: Yes, we have met. I participated in several marches of the February 20th Movement But the problem of the February 20th Movement itself is that it became content being a movement of protests and not a movement of propositions. It's a movement that didn't succeed in opening itself up toward other forces that could mobilise, notably women, democrats who are not in traditional political parties, and the traditional left. There is the root of the problems they are experiencing today. The February 20th Movement played a very positive role in the beginning, and then it weakened. It stopped at being a movement of protests, instead of working on the democratic project itself by proposing solutions.

CS: I have the impression from your writing that you still remain optimistic about the future. Is that true, and if it is true, how do you manage to stay optimistic?

AL: I have personally been against what we call 'merchants of despair'. Despair is a kind of merchandise here in Morocco. There are political movements that feed off the despair of the people to recruit, to mobilise, to capture a part of public opinion. There is a golden rule that has long nourished my thought, my reflection and my action, that of the Italian Antonio

Gramsci. He spoke of the pessimism of reason and the optimism of the will. Despair serves no purpose for me. Even if I sometimes become disheartened, I cannot lower my arms because my word carries a certain weight in Morocco. Consequently, I want to keep a little window open for hope. What exactly is that open window for hope? It is the optimism of the will that allows movement and change even when conditions are difficult.

CS: I personally encountered Morocco for the first time through the writings of Westerners like the American Paul Bowles and the Spaniard Juan Goytisolo. There has been a long tradition of Westerners visiting Morocco and writing it. I would like to know if you, as a Moroccan, have found interesting insights in these texts. Do they inform your own writing in any way? Or instead, do you perhaps find a warped picture of Morocco?

AL: I have read these writers from intellectual curiosity, of course. But let's say, it's not the literature that moves me deeply. There are some very intelligent things in Paul Bowles, moreso in Juan Goytisolo. But of course that cannot replace the view from the inside. We read these texts with interest as Italians, French, and Americans would read works dealing with their society or placing a story in their country. Can that replace their own literature? I don't believe so.

CS: Will you ever write about France? You have lived here for thirty years now...

AL: Listen, frankly, even if I have lived in exile for a very long time, the matrix of my writing has remained unchanged, and that's my link to Morocco. Because I believe that every country needs to create its own narrative that will be inscribed in the collective memory. That right there is one of the major concerns of literature, whether Moroccan, American, or Chinese. The other concern is to make sure that the message, the humanist values of the little humanity to which we all belong, with which we share sufferings and hopes, may be transmitted to the great humanity. How do we make sure that Morocco gains access to the universal? How do Moroccan men or women function from the inside? What is it that animates them and outrages them? What are their dreams? What are their obsessions? What are their hopes? How do they see others? Morocco is a very young country when it comes to literature. We do not have a great literary tradition, in contrast to Syria, Iraq, or Egypt, for example. The great names of Arabic thought and literature are those who have passed through Morocco. They lived there a little, but we ourselves do not have a great literary tradition. It's an extraordinary opportunity to begin when there isn't a great deal behind us, to broach an unknown territory. It's a little like the Far West. It's a true challenge to be met.

CS: When you return from Morocco, what do you miss the most?

AL: What I miss perhaps is the anarchy. Moroccan reality is an anarchic reality in everyday life, but it is an anarchy where the human is also present. Moroccans are neither better nor worse than any other people. But the people are very spirited, very spontaneous. There is something very uninhibited in their behaviour. They speak to others very easily. They communicate amongst themselves very easily. You just have to come up to someone smiling for everything to go well. Here in France human relations are a little more distant... people protect themselves. As for the cuisine, I make Moroccan food myself here, French and international as well. So there's that. I'm a particular kind of Moroccan; I am a universal Moroccan. I am all that human culture has made of me, with its diversity and its pluralism. In my writing, I lay claim to the several elements of Moroccan identity: Arabo-Muslim, Amazigh – that is, Berber – African, Mediterranean, Jewish, Saharan, but also Western. Morocco in Arabic means 'The Setting Sun' – that is, the extreme West... and then there is Andalusia with which I have a particular relationship...

CS: Do you know the history of your family? Were they Arabs from Andalusia?

AL: There is a story within my family, on my mother's side. She spoke of the fact that they were exiled. So I suppose that their ancestors belonged to what we call the Moriscos, who were chased out of Spain at the end of the sixteenth century and beginning of the seventeenth. We do have that legend in our family... and I think there is some truth to it, but my mother didn't know much about it, being illiterate. She didn't know history. It was the memory of that move that was transmitted to her. And physically she was someone with white skin, blue eyes, etc.

CS: A few more questions to finish up: You have remarked on several occasions that poetry is a way to resist the commodification of culture. But for a great many people, poetry remains difficult – even perhaps too difficult.

AL: Poetry is difficult to read or difficult to write?

CS: I'm referring just to reading and appreciating poetry, to be interested in something that is not a prose narrative or a movie. A word that some of my friends use to describe my own interest is 'pretentious'. So suppose you were talking with someone, say a young Moroccan, who finds that poetry is difficult, even pretentious, what would you say to that person?

AL: I would say first of all that we didn't give that person an opportunity during his studies to discover poetry, that great art which in the history of literature has been fundamental. Critics and historians of literature know very well that poetry has always played a primary role in the renewing of language and of writing. Poetry for me is a laboratory of literature. Language moves there, it transforms itself, and so as a result it has an impact on other literary genres. If today young people find difficulties with poetry, it's because we simply haven't prepared them. We haven't cultivated from the beginning an appetite for poetry. Thus we can't reproach them for that.

CS: And that returns us to the question of education.

AL: Absolutely. It's a question of education. And culture dominates in that question. We have arrived at a moment where literature is reduced to the novel, because the novel is the only literary product where there is a commercial concern. If authors today only wrote poetry, they would be ruined authors, unable to live from their pen. If you really want to live from your work as a writer, you must publish a novel every two years. If you are a poet, you will need to have another job. That said, I can't complain too much about the situation. That marginality of poetry allows me more freedom. There isn't any pressure. The commercial concerns aren't there, and so poetry is a very valuable art for literature. Then there are things that can be expressed in poetry that cannot be expressed in novels, except if perhaps the novel-writer is also a poet.

CS: What is your opinion of Moroccan rappers? Are you familiar with Fnaire, H-Kayne, Don Bigg?

AL: Yes, a little.

CS: There is creativity there, an acceptance of the language, and a capacity of self-expression, but at the same time, it isn't exactly the poetry that you have just described.

AL: It is one of the forms of poetry today. Of course, there will be traditionalists, poetry fundamentalists, who are going to find that it's not up to snuff. But there are different registers and different ways of writing poetry. What bothers me a little is that in this new expressive form there is a return to tradition. There was a moment in the nineteenth century when we liberated ourselves from fixed forms and from versification. Poetry since has evolved considerably thanks to this freedom. And yet, paradoxically, these youths are returning to tradition. But of course, their poetry does not have the same objective or the same function, and it doesn't address the same public. It is a poetry that is political in the end, a poetry of combat. And that reminds me personally of other moments in time where feminist poetry, for example, emerged to defend the female identity and to fight against the oppression of women. It reminds me also of the writings of prisoners who denounced the universe of incarceration and political oppression. But I think that in the panorama of current poetry, rap has its place. What I regret personally is that there isn't more dialogue between classical poets, let's say, of modernity and those poets. I think there is a real interest in dialogue. Personally I have sought it out. I collaborated with a Belgian rapper of Moroccan origin named Rival. We worked together to see how what we both wrote could communicate, and we did a show together. I requested some of the rappers to read my texts, to see what it would produce.

CS: One last question. In your poetry there is a mixing and melding of the descriptive and prophetic aspects. We might say, a denunciation of the world today that is mixed into declarations of a world that is to come. Can you elucidate a little the relationship between the two?

AL: Yes, of course. There's something archaic in the function of the poet that we should never abandon. It's an archaic art. In poetry, we find the first expression of human emotions: anger, fear, doubt, etc. Human memory has been conveyed by poetry. And it's also true that in its original, almost archaic, function, there was something prophetic about it. At the time of the founding of Islam, for instance, poets were very poorly seen by those considered as adversaries of the Prophet. It's true that the function of poetry is at the centre of what I write. That's why my poetry is also oral: a poetry of orality. For me it's important to go meet the public, either here or in Morocco or elsewhere in the world. I am a speaker of poetry and I consider that oral dimension as fundamental. Poetry is not just written; it is also the spoken word.

*

CHRISTOPHER SCHAEFER received the Ezra Pound Award for Best Translation from the University of Pennsylvania for his translations of the Cuban poet Javier Marimón. His translation of Roland Rugero's *Baho* was published by Phoneme Media in 2015.

Acknowledgements

My thanks to Michael Schmidt for commissioning this collection and to the MacDowell Colony, where I worked on many of these translations. Thanks are also due to the editors of the following publications where some of these translations originally appeared: *Poetry London*, *Modern Poetry in Translation*, *Inventory*, and *Transition*, among others. *The Manhattan Review* nominated 'Life' for a 2015 Pushcart Prize, while *Asymptote* nominated 'Letter to My Friends Overseas' for a 2016 Pushcart Prize. I owe Sarah Maguire of the Poetry Translation Centre a great debt for first affording me the opportunity to translate Mr Laâbi's work in 2011 when I led a number of workshops on his poetry. The results of those efforts were later collected in the pamphlet *Poems*, which the PTC published in March 2013. Some of those poems were also reprinted in the PTC's anthology *My Voice: A Decade of Poems from the Poetry Translation Centre* (Bloodaxe, 2014). Christopher Schaefer's interview with Mr Laâbi first appeared in *The Quarterly Conversation*. Thanks also to English PEN for their support through a 'PEN Translates!' grant in relation to this book. Finally, I am very grateful to both Christopher Schaefer and Jim Moore for their enthusiastic support throughout the process, as well as for their highly valuable contributions.

A N–S

Index of Titles